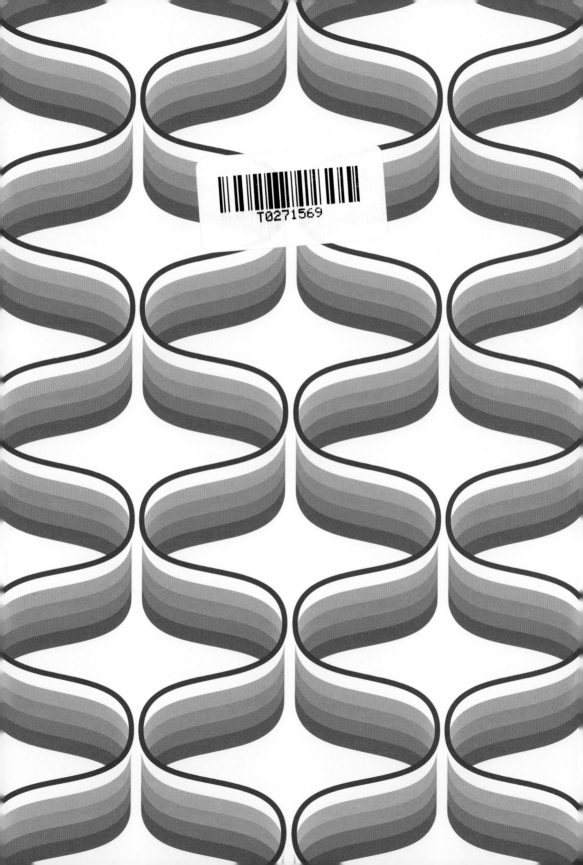

T0271569

An Hachette UK Company
www.hachette.co.uk

First published in Great Britain in 2023
by Kyle Books,
an imprint of Octopus Publishing Group Limited
Carmelite House
50 Victoria Embankment
London EC4Y 0DZ
www.kylebooks.co.uk

ISBN: 9781914239694

Distributed in the US by Hachette Book Group,
1290 Avenue of the Americas,
4th and 5th Floors, New York, NY 10104

Distributed in Canada by Canadian Manda
Group, 664 Annette St., Toronto, Ontario,
Canada M6S 2C8

Publisher: **Joanna Copestick**
Junior Commissioning Editor: **Samhita Foria**
Design: **Helen Bratby**
Photography: **Brent Darby**
Production Manager: **Caroline Alberti**

Printed and bound in China

10 9 8 7 6 5 4 3 2 1

All prices given correct at the time of press

For Elaine and Bob

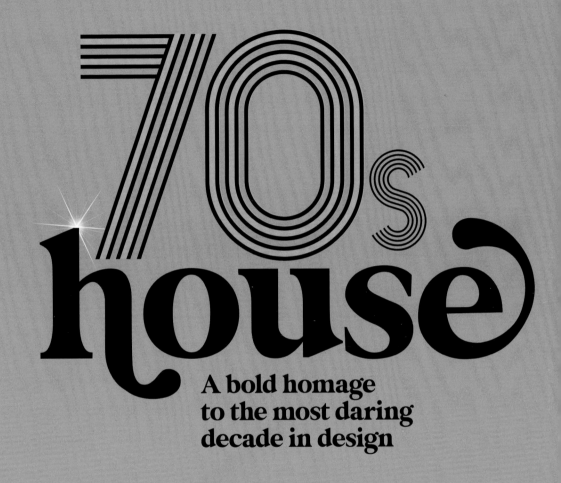

70s house

A bold homage
to the most daring
decade in design

ESTELLE BILSON

Photography by Brent Darby
Kyle Books

CONTENTS

FOREWORD
BARBARA HULANICKI

The world sees me foremost as a fashion designer – I am associated with fashion, of course, through Biba. But what many don't realize is that when it comes to fashion, interiors are just as important as clothes, in fact, interiors are a key part of fashion, both as a background to clothes and as a stage for the cultural zeitgeist.

Biba is rooted in vintage, inspired by antiques, of course, but back then in our twenties we couldn't afford that. Instead, it was down to World's End [an area in Chelsea, London] on a Saturday morning at 4am, where we would be found eagerly awaiting the arrival of trucks filled with vintage, V&A-museum-quality stuff piled high and sold cheap.

Biba evolved both with us and with our customers, from teens first leaving home and living in bedsits, to growing up and starting to have babies, moving into their first flats. Then our customers didn't just need clothes but home furnishings too. We only ever made necessities. We were a practical lifestyle brand. To me it was obvious to sell the very things I needed as I knew anything I needed my customers would also need. But practicality doesn't mean a lack of style. I was a working mother, so practicality came naturally; we brought out prams, furniture, homeware and even baked beans, all emboldened with Biba design and style.

In the Big Biba store, which opened in 1973, we created different room sets to give our customers ideas of how to style things. We would change it up often to keep things exciting. As we lived across from Kensington Palace in those days, I think Big Biba absolutely had a royal influence – I am a firm believer in taking influence from wherever you go.

My late husband, Fitz [Stephen Fitz-Simon], was inspiration for the shop décor. He absolutely hated going into shops with me, so since our very first Biba store, I made sure to have sofas for people to lounge on. The atmosphere we created in our stores was like a living room, a relaxed, comfortable environment. All the girls would bring their boyfriends, the shop would be filled with celebrities and musicians, everyone would feel comfortable.

Kids that age were living away from home for the first time, most of them in tiny bedsits. They'd say our shops were better than being at home, as they were opulent with lots of pillows and cushions – things they certainly didn't have in their own homes.

Back in those days, you didn't buy stuff for your house, instead it was handed down and you inherited all your furniture. It was only in the 60s and 70s, with the impact of Habitat, that people started to take more of an interest in homeware and have more control in their own home décor.

I think Estelle and 70s House Manchester is the next Habitat – it is the most important creative look since Conran. It is brilliant because it gives people the courage to use products without fear. On Instagram, where 70s House Manchester first launched, Estelle let people into her home which was filled with colour and amazing furniture. As she boldly showed us the inside of her home, even the bath water, it made me laugh, but also respect the openness of inviting the world inside.

One thing I find fabulous about 70s House Manchester is all the orange, because back in my Big Biba days orange was an absolute no-no! Interiors were inspired by Victorian colours – mushy plums and purples, dark, rich shades – as were the clothes. When I first saw the book, I thought wow, look at all that amazing furniture and treasure collected over many years. It is the opposite of what we see in magazines and TV, homes with no chutzpah, no individuality. Instead, this book acts as a guide, it shows how to use colour and pattern, how to search for your own vintage pieces and most importantly how to bring your own personality into your home. Estelle is an authority on 70s style and this book will show you step by step how to bring that style into your own home.

Love

Barbara

"Absolutely incredible, the designs of the wallpaper are super... it's not just one room, it's your whole house - the bathroom, my god!"

about Estelle

I was born in the east of England, the daughter of a cabinet maker and small-time antiques dealer. Furniture was always around me, from pieces my father bought and restored and going to junk shops and auctions. I knew how to clean down a band saw by the age of four, and artisans such as silversmiths and upholsterers were common visitors. I had always loved interiors; my doll's house never really had dolls in it, but I was constantly decorating and making new pieces for it, cutting pictures from magazines, or making a faux polar bear rug for in front of the fire. It is fair to say that I had extreme illusions of grandeur.

As a young child, our holidays were centred around what antiques shops and jumble sales there were locally. Many a time we would come home with items strapped to the roof rack or balanced and packed around us kids on the back seat; we looked like the Clampetts from *The Beverly Hillbillies*. But my dad always said, 'Where there is a will, there is a way', a motto that I also stand by when collecting furniture, and one which has made me laugh on more than one occasion as my own son has since been packed in around various finds in the back of the car. My partner sighs, rolls his eyes, and gets on with putting our own bargains on the roof rack.

Growing up in our family, either you were bored stiff, or you got with the programme and started collecting yourself. Items from the 60s and 70s were widely available in charity shops, auctions and at jumble sales, and my sister even worked for a time for an auctioneer's, so occasionally I would be able to get my grubby paws on unsold items from the general household auctions that people had asked to be disposed of: kitsch Tretchikoff-style chalkware lamps of glamorous ladies, old records, the lot.

My first forays into retro interior design came from trying to turn my teenage bedroom into what a 13-year-old thought was a version of the fashion store Biba, with ostrich feathers in vases and palm plants. My parents had lived in London in the swinging 60s and early 70s – my mum worked for an interior design company on Kensington Church Street and visited Biba in her lunch hour, while my dad was production manager for a furniture company in Fulham that worked with ex-service men. They recounted combined tales of hedonistic parties, fabulous shops and watching amazing bands. They even saw Jimi Hendrix perform in 1967 when my dad was at Leicester College of Art. My mum remembers Hendrix wearing a red military coat and playing guitar with his teeth, while my dad laments about someone 'nicking his best embroidered waistcoat'. When prompted they both would tell you about their 60s and 70s make-do-and-mend attitude to interior design, where they bought antiques to mix and match with contemporary items, such as using an old Union Jack flag as a bedspread, painting the bedroom ceiling sky blue, then gluing cloud shaped polystyrene ceiling tiles on it 'to cover the cracks', or pinning an Ingrid Boulting/Biba makeup poster in the loo. I emulated this as best I could using the £13.50 ($15) I earned per week in my first Saturday job. I bought huge paper lanterns and coloured light bulbs – I remember my mum being nonplussed about the red one; and I didn't understand the seedy undertones of this lighting choice. I settled with a green one for a time, but even with the light on it was like I was living in a swamp. Incense wafted around – you could cut the air with a knife – while I wore cotton hippie dresses and listened to music by Cat Stevens and Melanie, taken from my parent's vinyl collection, on my battered hi-fi. Naturally I was derided at school for the most part, labelled odd and weird due to my clothing and musical choices, preferring George Harrison and Jim Morrison over Bros and New Kids on the Block as my pin ups.

By the time I reached university, fortunately I met like-minded fans: we dressed in clothes from the 70s, listened to music from that decade and foraged the sides of roads, skips, tips and charity shops for furniture and accessories to decorate our dingy student digs. We hauled home teak sideboards found in skips; ate our dinners off Denby pottery, found for £1 ($1.30) in the Salvation Army shop; and put mass-market classic artworks on our walls. We skipped classes to go to rummage sales, and to barter with the eccentric second-hand shop owner of Scrooge on the Kettering Road, Northampton. There we found the best/worst taste items of clothing and accessories that we could. This was a time before eBay, before vintage clothing and homeware became glamorous and trendy – to us, it was second-hand. 'Mid-century', an interiors term that was coined in the late 80s, started to grow slowly as a trend. This seemed far too serious and grown up for us, we instead opted for shag pile and crazy purple curtains, hunted for lava lamps and beaded curtains – what others considered bad taste. I remember this time fondly, as the halcyon days of finding cheap and cheerful retro goodies – to us it was bright, fun and nostalgic – we loved it. To others it was junk, but to us it was gold.

Student life for the most part was good, apart from the cellar of our student digs, which we drew short straws to go in with the plagues of wasps, rats and hedgehogs (it's a long story). We went to soul nights in Northampton and Birmingham, and I made lifelong friends through our combined love of retro fashion and music. The mid-90s was a time of Brit Pop, but also one of the first retrospectives of 60s and 70s subcultures. My friends were mods, skins, punks and hippies – the outcasts, the dreamers, the artists, the visionaries. We didn't want to fit in, we wanted to be different and this is how we achieved it. I finally felt like I belonged and that I was no longer the odd one out. As I write this, I can remember quite clearly our homes, and our clothes, some of which were carelessly lost in the mists of time, and some pieces that I still own and cherish almost 30 years on. Sadly, so few photos of all this exist, in a time before the advent of social media and before people documented their lives, homes and even their dinners on their phones. I am partly sad about the lack of photographs of some of my formative years, but also incredibly grateful that my many faux pas have not been committed to the internet for eternity.

Graduating in fashion and then working for over 20 years in the luxury fashion industry as a technical designer and product developer, and latterly as head of technical design for one of the royal tailors on Savile Row, I watched how fashion and interiors often mirrored themselves. Trends came and went, inspired by interiors; and interiors that were inspired by fashion. While the rest of the world was looking at minimalist interiors or shabby chic in the 00s, in my own home I was still hoarding G Plan, bemoaning people who 'ruined' vintage furniture by painting it. I was putting heavily patterned wallpaper up and painting walls turquoise, or trying to play it cool when I came across a framed Tretchikoff's *Balinese Girl* in a house clearance for a few pounds. Friends would look to me when clearing out their grandparents' homes, and I would fill my car and home with their unwanted cast-offs while they affectionately joked that I had 'pensioner chic'. Almost 30 years later, I am sat in our home, surrounded by the product of three decades of collecting, reading, learning, honing my taste and switching out furniture for a better 'upgrade'. Most people assumed my love of orange and swirls would have diminished by my forties, but here I am, with a greater understanding and passion for the decade of style that I fell in love with in my teens. It never occurred to me that the way I decorated my home was unusual, it was just something I loved: being surrounded by happy, meaningful pieces which fill me with

nostalgia. Friends urged me to share my interiors on social media which led to people inquiring about using the house as a location for fashion shoots and, much to my surprise, it snowballed. People wanted to know where I bought my furniture, where to source wallpaper, fabrics, accessories, and suddenly people were interested in our home style and wanted it in their homes too. Historically, two of the items I struggled to find in great quantity were wallpaper and fabrics. It dawned on me one day that there was a gap in the market, and that if I loved these things, and other people wanted them too, then why didn't I make them? I was, after all, a product developer at heart, and interiors weren't that dissimilar to fashion, surely? A hobby soon became a self-funded brand based on a hairbrained idea. After a year, the collection of wallcoverings and fabric is now complemented by home accessories such as art prints, cushions, tea towels, candles and, my personal favourite, Christmas decorations, and is expanding rapidly. The designs are all unapologetically bold, bright and screamingly 70s in design – all inspired by the decade I love. Products within the range are currently sourced within the UK, focusing on north-west England and local, independent, ethical family businesses are used where possible. Our home continues to be available to hire as a location for film, photography and television, and I have been dubbed the 'go-to' 70s-style expert, featuring in the national and global press. I am also a regular specialist dealer on BBC's *The Bidding Room*, presented by national treasure Nigel Havers. When I look back over my life so far, no one is more surprised than me as to where my love of orange has taken me…

@70shousemanchester
www.70shousemanchester.com

Why the 70s?

WELCOME TO THE 70S!

Some may suggest that this was the decade that taste forgot, but scratch under the surface of the shag pile and you will find the most amazing, beautiful and memorable interior and product design.

The purpose of this book is to inspire and not dictate to you. This is an ideas book for you to take elements of areas you love and translate them into your own home. There are no rules to decorating, contrary to what people will tell you. Your home and style are unique and personal to you and what you love. This book will not tell you what palette is on trend or how to decorate, but it will open your eyes and senses to a whole world of glorious colour, texture, pattern, design, and aspects from the era to pick and choose from and call your own. The home layouts are not only loaded with ideas and tips but also prove that you don't necessarily need an unlimited budget to be able to achieve this retro style.

The first question people always ask me, Why the 70s? My answer is usually, Why not..? For me it is one of the most stylistically diverse decades, with everything from the clean lines of the late 60s and early 70s space-age inspired designs, through art deco-

inspired Big Biba, Disco and Studio 54, past Laura Ashley and what would now be termed 'cottage core', and landing up with punk. To deride the 70s as the decade that taste forgot is lazy, heaping together ten years into one homogenous brown lump.

You can open any history book or look online and find accounts of the decade: I could write a piece about the well-known social and political movements, about how the 70s was in fact the start of modern consumerist culture; I could write about the three-day week, the power shortages, piles of rubbish in the street, soaring costs, racism and feminism. It was politically a tumultuous decade. It would be fair to say that I enjoy vintage style, not vintage values.

But these aren't my memories of the 70s, not what inspires me with my home and style today. I was born in the 70s and my earliest memories are of brown walls, rya rugs and my dad playing The Moody Blues' 'Nights in White Satin' on vinyl. I remember listening to the *Grease* soundtrack on the radio while sitting on a potty, and the warm and simple comforts of home and my parents. Our house wasn't standard set up, we lived adjoining my father's workshop and still, to this day, the smells of certain varnishes and lacquers remind me of my youth. We didn't have a fancy home, it was simple, a basic conversion, with an outside toilet, it was dry and mostly warm, and I never remember wanting more. I partially attribute

my longing and nostalgia for the late 70s to the fact that our home at that time flooded out and I was, along with my family, made homeless. For me, the loss of items at a young age grew into a longing to replace what was once there, but this has since evolved into a passion for collecting that is not purely from a perspective of familiarity and comfort. This is not to say that I had an unhappy childhood, but, as for most people growing up in that decade, it wasn't easy.

Some of my earliest memories of interiors I was familiar with were relics of the 60s and 70s. While this era can be considered to be the start of modern consumerist culture, people still bought and kept their furniture, often for decades, unlike the wasteful generation we have become, where Instagram influencers seem to decorate every few weeks for sponsored content. My grandparents' houses, both maternal and paternal, were perfect examples of this, sources of great interest and conflicting styles. My paternal grandparents had moved into their new home post war, which was a typical council house with coloured Marley floor tiles, and small gardens to the front and rear. It had an early built-in kitchen and utilitarian bathroom. My father's parents had gone big on teak during the late 60s, and it was very much in their style to buy what was fashionable and the best they could afford. The furniture was much revered by my slightly domineering grandmother, Ada, who ritualistically cleaned it with teak oil and proudly set up the sideboard and gateleg table with black vinyl chairs and produced strange culinary concoctions for Sunday lunch. She was much like an unskilled Fanny Cradock - one could never tell what you were actually eating - who, almost in caricature would shout at my henpecked, pipe-smoking grandfather, Charlie, declaring at every meal that they needed a new tin for the Yorkshire pudding, blaming shoddy manufacturing, and not stopping to think that her dubious cookery was to blame. In contrast to this very formal, overbearing and 'look don't touch' set up, my maternal grandparents were an absolute dream. Where Ada ruled with iron, Reg and Hannah operated on an entirely different level. Theirs was a home of the wonderous, bizarre, homemade and, most importantly to me as a young and impressionable child, kitsch. They had a brown and orange bouclé sofa, a heavily patterned floral carpet, faux onyx tables with sleek chrome legs, a giant flokati-style rug (called Hairy Mary), Rumtopf West German pottery vases, huge 70s lights and corner shelves full of unusual Murano glass picked up on their travels around the world. I admired their sunburst clock in the dining room, remember the net curtains and mass-market art, and lament their perfectly manicured front garden, with rows of gladioli carefully tended. They had flock wallpaper in burnt gold, something so tactile that you could stroke it, and an avocado bathroom suite. Reg and Hannah were the bees' knees in my eyes: they were fun, exotic and ever so slightly bonkers. It is fair to say that they had a huge impact on me in different ways. Reg, a painter and decorator by trade, is responsible for me learning to wallpaper, almost by osmosis, studying him carefully as a child with his white decorator's overalls on, a Woodbine in his mouth and flat cap on his head. Hannah, on the other hand, would have been a modern-day stylist. She had no qualms about swapping rooms and furniture around, with gay abandon, hunting down treasure in charity shops and making home furnishings from everyday objects, known colloquially as 'mackeling' – my mother attributes my habits to Hannah's genes.

Some have called our home a tribute to the 70s but, in fact, most ordinary people would not have lived like this in the 70s. If you open a vintage interiors book from the era, or flick through a 70s magazine, most enduring images of the decade offer a skewed look as to how the average person decorated their home. Theirs would have been a mix of items from years past, and a hodge-podge of styles much like that of my own grandparents' and parents' homes. People rarely embraced a full-on look; this was usually the preserve of the rich and famous or interior designers and architects.

It is fair to say that how we have chosen to decorate our home is not the norm for most people and yes, it is on the extreme side of collecting. Our location home, 70s House Manchester, is therefore a whimsy, picking and choosing various aspects of retro and 70s design that appealed directly to my senses. It is a fantasy of what I would want a home to look like, my take on an imaginary 70s interior, an escapism from today's grey mediocrity, a nod to the nostalgia of my youth, and perhaps a desperate need to recreate that comfort and security of home as a child? It is not intended to be a tribute, or a pastiche or even an accurate representation of the era, mostly because I don't want my home to be covered in wood chip and to smell of cigarettes.

I needed our home to be fresh and relevant, and fit for life in the twenty-first century. I adore the styling and design of the 70s era, but I also needed to make it work for me and my family today. I have no desire to live in a museum, or a home so filled with all kinds of 'things' from the decade that it looks like an overfilled junk shop. With a young child and a cat, I don't want to be too precious about our collection that it interferes with our day-to-day life, I want to enjoy the playing and painting that goes hand in hand with family life. For us, and our child, there is nothing out of the ordinary of living in a house full of quality second-hand pieces. It is hard however, as an appreciator and collector, to differentiate the intrinsic value of a piece with what it was initially designed for, and that was to be used and lived with and enjoyed.

All the books and magazines that I own from the decade show beautifully styled homes with expensive Italian furniture, high-end lights and accessories. The gardens are manicured, with equally stylish people in evening attire enjoying cocktail parties. Then, as now, these are the things that people aspired to, but they aren't real life. Real life is buying on a budget, buying the best that you can afford at the time and sometimes living with things that aren't quite perfect. It also means that items are of significance – a book, a cherished toy or an ornament that might not fit into a sterile design but means the world to you. Sure, my space-age looking Keracolor TV might have been designed in 1968 (going on sale in 1970). Our sofa, despite being incredibly modern-looking, is in fact from 1975; the modular Ladderax units date from the mid-70s; the marble dining table from the late 70s – this is a mishmash of items I have found over the 30 years since I first started collecting, but somehow, they work. My home may not suit a purist but it is a reflection of the items that I enjoy and want to have around me. I believe they work because I love them. When people ask me what to look for and buy, I only ever advocate buying things you love, as at the end of the day you are the ones living with these pieces.

Buying second-hand is to us a way of life, it has become so ingrained in the way we are that we rarely buy new; it's not that we couldn't buy new, we just choose not to. Where once buying second-hand was the cornerstone of classism, a marker of those less able to afford new (a concept that was turned upon its head, ironically, in the 70s), it is now one of privilege as a result of the increased interest in all things retro and the subsequent gentrification of the concept of 'vintage'.

Over the years I've bought and sold furniture, replacing existing pieces with something different when I fancied a change, and upgrading when I saw the chance of selling one thing to afford another.

> "Have nothing in your houses that you do not know to be beautiful or believe to be useful."
> **William Morris**

One of the greatest things about buying pre-loved homewares is that you rarely lose money on an item of furniture or an accessory. I have also found, over the years, that a lot of high-street retailers copy vintage style, but rarely vintage quality. Every year in the UK we throw out around 9 million tonnes (10 million tons) of furniture, most of which is either incinerated or buried in landfill sites. By preserving and reusing this furniture, we can help to conserve the environment and its valuable resources, not to mention that using pre-existing furniture helps the circular economy of vintage dealers, creating employment for all manner of experts from house-clearance specialists, furniture restorers and upholsterers.

Our home isn't an expansive split-level mid-century, nor a mansion; it is a well-proportioned, humble end-of-terrace house. It was built at the turn of the twentieth century, and is typical of Manchester and much of the UK. The success of how I have chosen to decorate the house is that its roots lie very firmly in the 70s but it is still modern, relevant and it doesn't look like I live in a junk shop. Editing is everything. I have been guilty of piling it high and buying everything I can find and then lumping it all together, however it is the editing and styling that gives you that polished look.

What I have achieved is a relatable home, one where I hope you can look at the photographs and think that, with paint and a little imagination, you could achieve something similar. You might go from buying a vintage sofa on eBay to finding your own cohesive retro style by rummaging at your local vintage store or car boot sale.

70s House will enable you to transform a room so that it is relatable yet retro – a swanky pad to impress your friends and family and above all to relax and entertain in.

70s style overview

One of the things I have touched upon is the fact that the ten years from 1970 to 1979 were incredibly diverse with adopted styles. This is one of the reasons that I love the 70s; out of all of the previous decades, and those that followed, it has been a melting pot of style and design and one that people still take huge amounts of inspiration from, in terms of design, interiors and fashion nearly 50 years later.

So, what were the main styles of the 70s? As with all fashion and design, things evolve gradually and subtly over a period of time – no one suddenly changed everything to black ash furniture at the turn of midnight 1979!

The 70s were the beginning of the end of 'mid-century modern' design. Even though the decade is occasionally amalgamated into the mid-century timeline, the modern aspect of mid-century where architects and interior designers sought out simplistic designs based on functionality and elegance during the post-war period of the 50s and 60s, is certainly not the most recognized 70s aesthetic. The 70s took the mid-century modern design principles, turned them on their head, cranked the volume up and brought back ornamentation to interior design that hadn't been since the turn of the century.

At the start of the decade, we saw a hangover from the halcyon days of the late 60s, with its flower power and swirling, acid-soaked designs and psychedelia. Hippie styling and the free love culture was still very much prominent right through the decade along with the new self-sufficiency movement.

The first Earth Day was observed on 22 April

1970, which was a chance to highlight how mass consumerism was damaging our planet, something we still seem to be struggling to grasp more than half a century on. Materials such as bamboo and rattan and crafts such as macramé and crochet were popular, eschewing the bigger, bolder, louder styles of the two previous decades. It was a chance for people to step back and understand how they were consuming, and look at how their surroundings and products impacted the Earth. As a result, more natural colours such as muted greens, golds and browns became popular, and these colours form part of the cornerstone of 70s design.

In complete contrast to this natural and holistic approach to design and life was the graphic modernism style and space-age, plastic fantastic chic that was popularized in the 60s. Eero Aarnio's 'Ball Chair', ultramodern egg chairs and tulip chairs and tables, although designed in the 50s and 60s, were still ever present within 70s style and design. This bright, white, futuristic styling continued well into the 70s and morphed into the clean and minimal chrome and glass that became ubiquitous in the late 70s and into the 80s.

During the latter part of the 60s and the early part of the 70s, we saw a generation enthralled by styles prominent in the early years of the twentieth century, with art nouveau influencing psychedelia. This coincided with an exhibition at the Victoria and Albert Museum in 1966 by British illustrator Aubrey Beardsley, famous for his black ink drawings. Looking at Sanderson fabrics and wallpapers from their 1972 Palladio range, you can clearly see the art nouveau influence coming through with designs

such as 'Nana' by Pat Etheridge, which have a decidedly Alphonse Mucha vibe to them. These were originally designed in 1968 for their Triad range of co-ordinating wallpapers and fabrics, but the depiction of a nude woman was considered too risqué even for the late 60s. It is no coincidence that both traditional Sanderson designs and William Morris designs had a resurgence during the decade.

Art deco was incredibly in vogue, made popular by Barbara Hulanicki and the last of the Biba stores, Big Biba, which opened in 1973 and finally closed its doors in 1975 (see page 34). The iconic logo of the legendary New York nightclub Studio 54 (1977–80) is also art deco-style, basking in the elegance of an earlier time of old Hollywood glamour and extravagance.

By the end of the decade people were enthralled by the likes of Laura Ashley and her homespun look based on the style of British illustrator Kate Greenaway. Stripped pine Georgian and Victorian interiors lent themselves to those buying old Victorian properties that were being refurbished, and original features that had been ripped out under DIY expert Barry Bucknell's instruction 20 years earlier, began to be reintroduced.

Some of the most enduring memories of 70s interiors are, of course, the bright oranges, purples and brown (lots of brown). Wood in all sorts of finishes from natural teak to plastic laminate on fridge doors; bright and bold wallpaper and fabrics; dark mood lighting and shag pile carpets; these are the sorts of items that have captured the spirit of the decade in the minds and hearts of those that were there or long to be there.

One of the main things that continually brings me back to the 70s as a source of inspiration is that there has never been a decade where so many contrasting and polar opposite styles existed, separated by subcultures, age and demographic. At one end of the spectrum, you have people buying 'antiques' from junk shops and living a bohemian lifestyle in louche bedsits, people subscribing to the 'Good Life' ethos of self-sufficiency and trying life 'off grid', versus middle class or aspiring middle class buying mock Georgian furniture and very traditional styles such as the Parker Knoll 'Penshurst' chair, which has been in constant production for over 70 years. The middle aged, who favoured sensible and practical furniture that was built to last and seen as an 'investment', were juxtaposed with young professionals buying into chic Italian design with its smoked glass, leather and chrome.

One of my favourite source books from the period is the 1974 style bible *The House Book*, by Terence Conran. A quick flick through the pages will show clearly the extent of variety from farm and town houses to international, Mediterranean and eclectic styles.

This melting pot of styles and design influences from culture, fashion, interiors and music, means that there is no real right or wrong way to style your 70s home. You can take as many elements as you please from various reference points through the decade. However, there will always be certain aspects that make a home instantly recognizable as retro or 70s in style. Should you wish to include these to create an instant impact, they can be found in the 10 key looks section on page 98.

"The best rooms have something to say about the people who live in them." DAVID HICKS

FINDING 70s
INSPIRATION

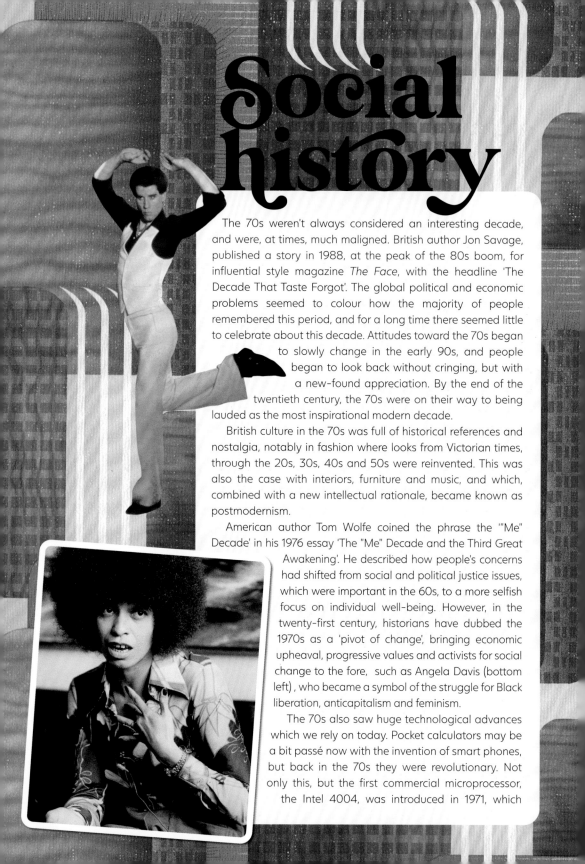

Social history

The 70s weren't always considered an interesting decade, and were, at times, much maligned. British author Jon Savage, published a story in 1988, at the peak of the 80s boom, for influential style magazine *The Face*, with the headline 'The Decade That Taste Forgot'. The global political and economic problems seemed to colour how the majority of people remembered this period, and for a long time there seemed little to celebrate about this decade. Attitudes toward the 70s began to slowly change in the early 90s, and people began to look back without cringing, but with a new-found appreciation. By the end of the twentieth century, the 70s were on their way to being lauded as the most inspirational modern decade.

British culture in the 70s was full of historical references and nostalgia, notably in fashion where looks from Victorian times, through the 20s, 30s, 40s and 50s were reinvented. This was also the case with interiors, furniture and music, and which, combined with a new intellectual rationale, became known as postmodernism.

American author Tom Wolfe coined the phrase the '"Me" Decade' in his 1976 essay 'The "Me" Decade and the Third Great Awakening'. He described how people's concerns had shifted from social and political justice issues, which were important in the 60s, to a more selfish focus on individual well-being. However, in the twenty-first century, historians have dubbed the 1970s as a 'pivot of change', bringing economic upheaval, progressive values and activists for social change to the fore, such as Angela Davis (bottom left), who became a symbol of the struggle for Black liberation, anticapitalism and feminism.

The 70s also saw huge technological advances which we rely on today. Pocket calculators may be a bit passé now with the invention of smart phones, but back in the 70s they were revolutionary. Not only this, but the first commercial microprocessor, the Intel 4004, was introduced in 1971, which

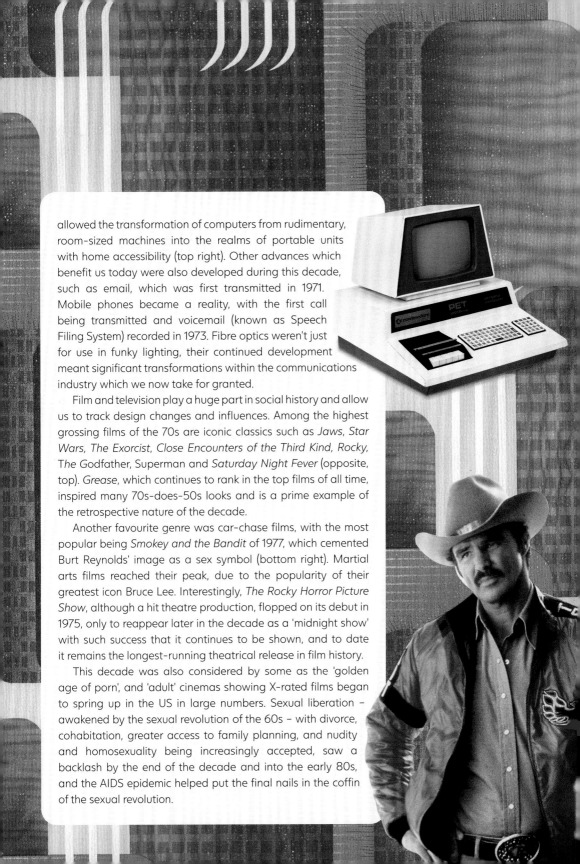

allowed the transformation of computers from rudimentary, room-sized machines into the realms of portable units with home accessibility (top right). Other advances which benefit us today were also developed during this decade, such as email, which was first transmitted in 1971. Mobile phones became a reality, with the first call being transmitted and voicemail (known as Speech Filing System) recorded in 1973. Fibre optics weren't just for use in funky lighting, their continued development meant significant transformations within the communications industry which we now take for granted.

Film and television play a huge part in social history and allow us to track design changes and influences. Among the highest grossing films of the 70s are iconic classics such as *Jaws*, *Star Wars*, *The Exorcist*, *Close Encounters of the Third Kind*, *Rocky*, The *G*odfather, Superman and *Saturday Night Fever* (opposite, top). *Grease*, which continues to rank in the top films of all time, inspired many 70s-does-50s looks and is a prime example of the retrospective nature of the decade.

Another favourite genre was car-chase films, with the most popular being *Smokey and the Bandit* of 1977, which cemented Burt Reynolds' image as a sex symbol (bottom right). Martial arts films reached their peak, due to the popularity of their greatest icon Bruce Lee. Interestingly, *The Rocky Horror Picture Show*, although a hit theatre production, flopped on its debut in 1975, only to reappear later in the decade as a 'midnight show' with such success that it continues to be shown, and to date it remains the longest-running theatrical release in film history.

This decade was also considered by some as the 'golden age of porn', and 'adult' cinemas showing X-rated films began to spring up in the US in large numbers. Sexual liberation – awakened by the sexual revolution of the 60s – with divorce, cohabitation, greater access to family planning, and nudity and homosexuality being increasingly accepted, saw a backlash by the end of the decade and into the early 80s, and the AIDS epidemic helped put the final nails in the coffin of the sexual revolution.

FUN FACT

Fred Finn is the world's most-travelled Concorde passenger, flying a whopping 718 times.

Travel

Although package holidays had become more popular and affordable since the 50s and 60s, it was the 70s when international travel really took off, with the first Pan Am Boeing 747 jet landing at Heathrow in 1970. This type of 400-seater jet plane offered huge economies of scale, making it affordable to go anywhere in the world, and making trans-Atlantic travel accessible to people without extreme wealth for the first time.

From the UK, holidays to Spain continued to be popular, with the construction of high-rise tourist cities sprouting up from once charming villages, such as Benidorm, to cater for the holidaymakers. This was encouraged by dictator General Franco, who saw tourism as a way of bringing money into what he considered a 'backward' nation. Spain boomed with the jet plane capacities and 2-hour non-stop flights from UK airports for the 'pile it high, sell it cheap, sun and sangria' holiday, that was until 1974 when thousands of holidaymakers were stranded during the first global oil crisis.

The rich and famous might have wanted to take advantage of the ultimate in luxury – a trip on the supersonic airliner, Concorde, which ran commercial flights between 1976 and 2003. This high-tech airliner flew from London to New York in under 3 hours, for those who could pay the $1,500 round trip (about $7,600 in today's money). Notable passengers included Dolly Parton, Mick Jagger and Calvin Klein. Paul McCartney would take along his guitar and sing songs while Andy Warhol would routinely leave with pieces of the specially designed Raymond Loewy cutlery.

For those not able to stretch to the Costa del Sol, then a bucket and spade holiday in Blighty would be the order of the day, either on a static caravan park (maybe with a Spa shop) or a Butlin's or Pontins at one of the many sites around the UK. For more on Butlin's, check out our kitsch section on page 77.

Television

Seventies television has always had a huge impact on me, from watching *Top of the Pops* with my mum every Thursday night to enjoying endless reruns of classic films and comedies. It formed a huge part of my interest in the decade from an early age. I have fond memories of children's television, which seemed much more gentle, colourful and simple than anything produced nowadays. I have memories of watching programmes with my family such as *The Muppet Show*, *Dr Who*, which was at its peak in the 70s (I was always watching behind a cushion), *Wonder Woman*, played by Lynda Carter, and *The Dukes of Hazzard*, which was released in 1979.

In the UK, all three channels were broadcasting in colour by 1969. However, colour TV sets in UK homes didn't outnumber black-and-white ones until 1976, mainly due to the cost. Ninety-three per cent of homes had access to a television, with many people renting sets from companies such as Rumbelows. (We didn't have a colour television until later in the 80s, but my maternal grandparents bought a set specifically to watch the wedding of Charles and Diana in 1981 and a large group of us sat around to watch the spectacle in full technicolour.)

Comedy was the king of British television during this decade with some of the most well-loved series being produced. They were repeated heavily over the years and lauded as classic television, from the camp *Are You Being Served?*, with catchphrases such as 'I'm free!', to *Porridge*, with the fabulous Ronnie Barker (one half of popular 70s sketch show *The Two Ronnies*, with Ronnie Corbett) playing the habitual criminal, Norman Stanley Fletcher, aka Fletch, who is serving a five-year sentence in prison. Each episode focuses on the inmates' time in prison and the various comedic scrapes they endure. Others that rank on the list of best comedies of all time include *Fawlty Towers*, with John Cleese as manic hotelier Basil Fawlty and Prunella Scales as his overbearing wife,

Yootha Joyce

Our best-selling design is named Yootha after Yootha Joyce, the actress best known for playing Mildred Roper in *Man about the House* and *George & Mildred*. Her image also appears on the sleeve of The Smiths' 1986 single *Some Girls Are Bigger Than Others*.

Sybil, and *George & Mildred* (a spin-off from the earlier sitcom *Man about the House*) starring Brian Murphy and Yootha Joyce as the Ropers as a sparring middle-aged couple.

One of my absolute favourite sitcoms, and one of which I watch the Christmas special edition with almost religious zeal every year, is *The Good Life* (bottom), which ran from 1975 to 1978. It features Richard Briers having a mid-life crisis, quitting his job and deciding to go self-sufficient with his long-suffering, and beautifully doe-eyed wife, Barbara (Felicity Kendal). They convert their suburban home into a farm, much to the chagrin of social-climbing neighbours Margo and Jerry Leadbetter (Penelope Keith and Paul Eddington). Margo is played deliciously by Keith, on the surface a snobby, self-obsessed housewife, who teeters on the verge of a bully, yet beneath her fantastically elegant clothes (a reason alone to watch), she is an awkward, fragile character, who lacks confidence and suffers the triumphs and humiliations with great comedic effect, and which cements her in the hearts of all who have watched *The Good Life*. She is a elegant force to be reckoned with and, deep down, I think we all wish we were a little bit more like Margo.

Other television highlights that still live large in the collective unconscious when you mention the 70s are *Abigail's Party* (see page 170) and the bawdy seaside postcard humour of the highly popular *Carry On* series of films which ran between 1958 and 1978. Thirty films were released over this 20-year period, projecting actors such as Sid James, Kenneth Williams, Barbara Windsor, Terry Scott and June Whitfield (who later starred in the late 70s sitcom *Terry and June*) into the hall of comedy fame.

Music

When thinking about 70s music, disco automatically comes to mind. This, however, only became popular during the mid- to late 70s with performers such as Donna Summer (top left), the Bee Gees, ABBA and Village People. Disco is certainly one of the most enduring legacies of the decade from a music and style perspective, so much so that it influenced fashion, decor, New York nightclubs such as The Loft and Studio 54, and films such as *Saturday Night Fever*.

But the 70s were not only about disco. Popular music continued to be dominated by musicians and bands who had achieved notoriety in the 60s such as Bob Dylan, the Rolling Stones, Fleetwood Mac and the Grateful Dead, and newer singer-songwriters such as Elton John (opposite, bottom), Carole King and Kate Bush.

Rock became heavier with early heavy-metal artists Judas Priest, AC/DC, Led Zeppelin, Black Sabbath and Deep Purple producing harder-edged rock music. Glam rock also emerged in the early 70s with performers wearing exaggerated and flamboyant clothing and make up. David Bowie, as his alter ego Ziggy Stardust, personified this, along with bands T-Rex, Queen and Slade (who live on every year with their heavily played number one single 'Merry Christmas Everybody' and solo artists such as Suzi Quatro (bottom left).

Psychedelic rock was still popular with bands such as The Doors, who released their last album *L.A. Woman* in April 1971, three months before lead singer Jim Morrison's death. Alongside, there were prog rock bands such as Yes, Genesis and Pink Floyd, whose 1973 album *The Dark Side of the Moon* remained in the the charts for more than 741 weeks from 1973-88 in the UK but stayed for 962 weeks in the US Billboard charts, and remains one of the best-selling albums of the decade.

Prog rock in turn influenced European bands, such as Kraftwerk, as well as Roxy Music's Brian Eno, who is considered the father of ambient music, earning this accolade with his 1978 album *Music for Airports*.

Motown music became hugely popular with artists such as Stevie Wonder, Marvin Gaye and the Jackson 5 dominating the global charts, breaking down racial barriers and influencing future pop culture. In turn, Motown influenced the hip-hop culture, when New York block parties incorporated DJs playing funk and soul. In 1979, Sylvia Robinson and her husband Joe founded Sugarhill Records and put together a rap group called Sugarhill Gang, who released 'Rappers Delight', which became hip hop's first mainstream rap music hit. Pop music included the likes of The Osmonds, Bay City Rollers, Cher, Carly Simon, David Essex (top right) and Brotherhood of Man. There were even comedy acts such as The Wombles from the popular children's television series, as well as shmaltzy novelty songs like 'Grandad' by Clive Dunn.

Living in Manchester, Northern soul is something close to my heart, not only in stylings, but musicality. Northern soul peaked in northern England and the Midlands in the mid-70s, and celebrates a particular style of Black American soul music. The sub-culture evolved from the underground rhythm and soul scene in the late 60s in venues such as the Twisted Wheel in Manchester and by the 70s, the most well-known club was the Wigan Casino (1973-81). As the decade progressed, the beats became more up-tempo and Northern soul's iconic style of dancing became more athletic, featuring spins, karate-style kicks and complicated drops. Inspired by the Northern soul scene of the 60s and 70s, 70s House Manchester has its own version of the traditional Northern soul patch, featuring the red rose of Lancashire and Manchester's emblem, the worker bee.

The latter part of the decade saw punk rock emerge, an underground scene, until two bands, the Sex Pistols and the Ramones, made everyone take notice in 1976. Simply known as punk, it had its origins in 60s garage and rejected the excesses of mainstream rock. Prominent acts included the Buzzcocks, Patti Smith and the Clash. By 1977 the subculture had gone mainstream, helped by the manager of Sex Pistols and New York Dolls, Malcom McClaren, who, with then-girlfriend Vivienne Westwood, changed the course of music and fashion forever.

WHAT IS RETRO?

Items from the 70s are often described as retro, so what is this term and what does it mean?

Retro style imitates past trends, lifestyles and artforms, including fashion, music and interiors. The word itself is a derivative of the Latin prefix meaning backwards, or looking towards the past. Similar to the word 'retrograde', it implies gazing longingly towards the past instead of looking forward to the future. Interestingly, the modern usage of the word 'retro' itself was first recognized in 1972 and used on items that were new but mimicked previous eras.

Before the word retro was coined by the press the practice of looking back and adopting older styles was commonplace, the difference was that it was now being used to refer to the recent past. Generally, in popular culture, the cycle of nostalgia is approximately 20 to 30 years prior to the current one. The 70s saw many aesthetic influences, young people were looking back at the glamour of pre-war art deco and 50s Americana, with shops such as London's Mr Freedom and the 1978 blockbuster film *Grease*, which details the lives of strangely adult-looking students at Rydell High School.

Many put their own individual twist on these influences in clothing and interiors. Out of this grew the roots of the glam-rock look that was made popular by bands such as

Queen, T-Rex and Sweet. These colourful young things
could be found hawking around the end of Portobello Road
looking for second-hand items to furnish their studio flats
and first homes, in sharp contrast to the married 30- and
40-somethings who wanted smart, matching items from
G Plan and three-piece suites.

Up until the 60s, interior designers tended to decorate homes
with antiques. A cultural change in the late 60s and 70s,
however, meant that fashion boutiques such as London's I was
Lord Kitchener's Valet started selling military uniforms from
the turn of the century, and shops offered everyday second-
hand furniture. These were seen to differ from traditional
antiques shops and to many they simply sold 'junk'. Much was
the same when I started collecting 70s items in the 90s, and
this became a cyclical urge for the nostalgia of youth.

Many people now use the word 'retro' to refer to original
items of a certain period, most notably the 50s-70s. The notion
of retro interiors as a style of design now means one where
original items from the 50s, 60s and 70s are used to furnish
a home. In the last 20 years these artefacts from previous
decades have become more desirable and not commonplace
junk, and as a result, the word 'retro' not only means
something from the recent past but something of cultural or
monetary value.

Influential design

BIBA

When thinking about iconic stores in the 70s, one instantly thinks of Biba, the brain child of Barbara Hulanicki and her husband Stephen Fitz-Simon, which had humble beginnings as a postal boutique run from home. Barbara hit gold when she designed a sugar-pink gingham dress and matching headscarf, very much in the flavour of Brigitte Bardot, which was a roaring success, and she sold over 17,000 outfits.

Biba was my absolute first love; my mother worked around the corner from the store on Kensington High Street and would shop there during her lunch breaks. Sadly very little of what she bought survives today. I still remember my mum wearing Biba make up into the 80s, when it could be bought through the clothing store Dorothy Perkins. I first read Barbara Hulanicki's autobiography *From A to Biba* in my early teens, inspired by the opulence and attention to detail. I was so obsessed by this that I was inspired to move into the world of fashion myself.

There were several successive Biba stores in various locations around Kensington, each one larger and grander than the previous. Barbara curated the interiors to match the history of the shop, from Victorian chemists to their last incarnation, Big Biba, also dubbed 'The Most Beautiful Store in the World', which was positioned in the old Derry & Toms art deco department store, complete with a restaurant/nightclub and roof garden.

The Biba store was a mecca for anyone who was anyone. Everyday, people flooded to experience their unique stores, furnished with opulent fabrics and gold leaf, mixing in communal changing rooms with the stars of the day. Huge supporters included Twiggy, Mia Farrow, Cilla Black and Barbara Streisand. Even fashion behemoth Anna Wintour cut her teeth as a shop assistant and both Barbara and Stephen proudly hired young, approachable staff, who mirrored their customers, and who were never to approach people to try to make a sale. Shoppers flocked to experience the unique atmosphere that Biba exuded, with loud pop music that could be heard from the street, to sit and take it all in and shop among the antiques that were foraged to create their iconic dark and seductive interiors. Biba was a destination, with people outside London making special trips just to visit the store. During this period it was London's second most popular tourist attraction, after the Tower of London, and the third was Buckingham Palace.

The interior design of the stores, especially Big Biba, has always fascinated me. I studied pictures of the huge spaces, decked out in peach glass and marble, leopard print, art deco-inspired fabrics and lights (which you could of course buy, and I am lucky enough to own one). *Vogue* called it a palace with, coloured counters and seven floors of

ABOVE, JUSTIN DE VILLENEUVE PHOTOGRAPHS HIS THEN-PARTNER, TWIGGY, AS SHE LOUNGES SEDUCTIVELY ON THE CIRCULAR LEOPARD PRINT BED IN BIG BIBA, 1971. RIGHT, BIBA ART-DECO STYLE LAMP FROM THE BIG BIBA ERA, A LUCKY CAR-BOOT FIND FOR JUST A FEW POUNDS. FAR RIGHT, LONDON'S BIG BIBA STORE.

fantasy – each of these seven floors having its own identity and logo. Clothing hung on Victorian hat stands, which became a mainstay of their store designs. Scratching the surface, there were other quirky examples of design, such as a kitsch section to purchase naff but amusing home goods; their children's department in the basement with a cottage and toadstools was straight out of 30s Disney; humorous nods to pop art with oversized record players selling vinyl; and their food halls, a sight to behold, with produce being stocked in huge Campbells soup cans, à la Warhol, and pet food being supplied from the tummy of a giant Great Dane dog, modelled on Barbara's own pet, Othello,

with a cheeky fig leaf to protect his modesty.

The restaurant was named the Rainbow Room because of the huge, sweeping elliptical ceiling fitted with concealed neon-coloured lighting. Even the jacquard tablecloths and crockery were especially designed for this purpose – a black lustre glaze with gold art deco logo and a dancing couple. Design duo Steve Thomas and Tim Whitmore carefully restored the fabrication of the building back to its former glory, even down to recreating original carpets. The roof garden offered a tea room, the opportunity to relax on the grass and to take afternoon tea on specially commissioned Edwardian-style peacock chairs; there were even flamingos! In fact, everything was carefully branded, from homewares to glitter wellington boots; items from their logo shop, like packs of cards or colouring books, to a humble bottle of bleach from the food halls; everything was given the Biba star treatment – nothing was too mundane to be made fabulous. This is one of the reasons why the legacy of Biba has endured; neither before, nor since has there been such a concept store on such a huge scale.

"Biba was not merely a shop, it came to represent a complete philosophy, and for many the end of Biba marked the end of an era."
Sally Brampton, *Observer*, 1983

HABITAT

The man responsible for the success of duvets (or 'continental quilts' as they were called), chicken bricks, woks and affordable paper pendant light shades in the UK was Terence Conran and his Habitat store, which opened to market his range of Summa furniture – a sleek, modernist range of modular teak units.

Conran started his own design practice – The Conran Design Group – in 1957 with the vision of 'Plain, Simple, Useful' and introducing contemporary furniture and interiors to the post-war generation. He firmly believed that 'Design is there to improve your life'. He famously designed a store for British fashion designer Mary Quant.

Conran opened Habitat in 1964 on Fulham Road, Chelsea, and introduced a new and exciting way to purchase contemporary homewares in the UK with a distinctly European feel, inspired by visits to France. The store aesthetic featured whitewashed walls, white wood ceilings, red clay quarry tile flooring and spot lighting to make the product the star of the show. This was something that was unheard of at the time and the chain of stores expanded rapidly throughout the 60s and 70s. Conran attributes the success of his venture to inexpensive pasta storage jars; Habitat was one of the few places which sold these, just as the market for dry pasta took off in the UK. Such was the success of the business that it commissioned a collection of original prints from two of Britain's most important contemporary artists, David Hockney and Peter Blake.

The store was reported to be a deeply personal project for not only Conran, whose own home appeared in the first mail-order catalogue, but also for the managing director whose pet cat could be spotted in other, subsequent editions.

Habitat famously launched a successful mail-order business, Habitat By Post, in 1966, allowing people to shop remotely and buy into the store's lifestyle for the first time. By 1971, the way furniture was bought changed, with people starting to look towards flat-pack furniture from Habitat, where kits could be purchased to assemble from their 'take-away' racks, way before IKEA expanded into the UK and US in the 80s. The flat-pack revolution in the UK was spearheaded by Conran who had his own manufacturer in 1962 solely to produce flat-pack furniture (known then as knock-down furniture). This developed into their 'Housepack' service, which provided all the essential items needed to move straight into a three-bedroom house, all neatly packaged in a six-foot container. By the mid-70s, faced with recession, they offered a 'Basic Habitat' range, a collection of low-cost, entry-level products.

There are many recognizable designs that were sold in store which are still desirable today. One such piece is a bentwood and bergère cane chair called the 'Cesca', originally designed by Hungarian-American designer Marcel Breuer in 1928 and named as a tribute to his adoptive daughter, Francesca. These chairs have become incredibly sought after in recent years and their prices have rocketed as a result, despite them being later replicas of a Bauhaus design. Habitat also stocked Arkana-branded tables and chairs, as well as wire chairs by furniture designer Harry Bertoia.

By 1973, the success of Habitat meant that Conran was able to open the Conran Shop, an upmarket (more expensive) furniture and design shop, in the original Habitat location He also acquired the long-established Heal's department store in 1983. By the late 80s, Habitat was struggling due to the arrival of IKEA, and by the early 90s Conran had lost control of Habitat due to internal politics with the Storehouse Group who now owned the store. Habitat still exists today, owned as a trading name of Argos in the UK.

> **"Habitat brought well-designed items into people's homes before they knew what design was."**
> **Tord Boontje**

Throughout his career, Conran was not only a designer, but a notable restaurateur and author, writing over 50 books reflecting his design philosophy. His most famous, *The House Book* from 1974, is a hefty tome which covers everything you could ever need to decorate your own home with confidence. This book can still be bought second-hand relatively easily and cheaply, along with his follow-up titles: *The Bed and Bath Book* and *The Kitchen Book*. There are no surprises as to what these contain, but they still remain one of the best series of source books for the budding retrophile wanting to convey a sense of authenticity to their retro home. Every room is covered in exacting detail with chapters specifically for internal layouts, floors, walls, lighting and colour. If I were to recommend only one source book for people to start with, it would be *The House Book*.

1972 Annual Catalogue 20p

Top tip
Look out for the Conran range of 'Crayonne' objects, made from brightly coloured moulded plastic, including mirrors, ice buckets, house numbers and ashtrays, which have a distinctly minimalistic space-age vibe.

Before Conran "there were no chairs and no France."
Craig Brown

LEFT, TERENCE CONRAN.
RIGHT, THE 'CESCA' CHAIR.

G PLAN

In 1951, the Festival of Britain saw 8 million people visit the country. This dream world, very different from post-war Britain, was a celebration of early 50s style: bright, colourful and modern, without the seriousness of pre-war modernism. As the decade progressed, contemporary furniture evolved with lighter woods such as oak and beech, and with splayed and tapered legs. These simple, elegant pieces worked perfectly with the brightly coloured, abstract wallpapers and soft furnishings that were being designed and manufactured.

G Plan, which launched in 1953 by Donald Gomme, was a post-war revolution that changed attitudes to contemporary furniture, making design desirable and accessible. Up until this point it was relatively unheard of for furniture manufacturers to brand their own goods for resale. Not only did G Plan do just that but they took control of the aesthetics and advised retailers on how to present their ranges within their showrooms, which were laid out in room sets. The plan was to produce designs over a longer period of time so customers could not only buy or hire purchases but also save up for the mix-and-match pieces.

One of the brand's most enduring and prolific designs is the 'Fresco' range. Designed by V.B. Wilkins and introduced in 1966, the range was produced in teak wood in various designs until the mid- to late 70s. Standing out from the crowd with its simple lines, inspired by Scandinavian design, the iconic curved wooden handles are instantly recognizable. One of the benefits of this range was its modular system, whereby you could create a set of shelves and units as large or as small as your accommodation permitted. While this range is collectable, the earlier pieces are made from solid wood as opposed to the later pieces, which are made from veneer. V.B. Wilkins is also responsible for two of the most sought-after and iconic pieces of G Plan. The '8040' occasional table, often mistakenly referred to as the 'Astro' today by fans of retro furniture, was introduced in 1965 and has a distinctive glass top matched with swooping criss-crossed legs. A huge success, the company introduced an oval-shaped one in 1969. Released in November 1970, the 'Astro' is a different design, the only similarity being that both have glass tops. Often called the 'Spider', due to its many legs in an hourglass formation, this is a rare find and should be snapped up immediately if found in the wild. One of my favourite collections is the sleek, understated 'Form Five', designed by R. Bennett and produced for a limited time from the late 60s to 1970. Bennett was part of the in-house design team at G Plan and was responsible for the 'Quadrille' range.

Buyer Beware

✱ Some G Plan pieces are sold as part of the 'Kofod' range but aren't actually part of this collaboration. 'Kofod' pieces have a gold stamp with Danish designer Ib Kofod-Larsen's signature.

✱ Although it is possible to refinish these pieces, if they have watermarks please go carefully, the veneer is paper thin and you can easily sand through to the chipboard underneath, ruining your hard work.

✱ Do your homework, a lot of sellers label their items as G Plan, especially on online auctions, when they aren't. Ask to see the original label if it is a genuine G Plan item that you want to buy.

The early 70s became the heyday for the brand as the company's turnover grew substantially. As the decade moved on, several new ranges were launched, such as the 'Libretto' in 1973, which featured two-tone woods, chrome handles, backlit units and – a 70s essential – smoked glass. Modular seating became popular with chairs being sold with and without arms that could be connected into sofa seating. The 'Montage' was a short-lived design, available between 1977 and 1979. One thing that is notable is that G Plan never followed the trend for pine furniture that started to become increasingly popular, nor the contrasting ultra-modern tubular steel look that carried on into the 80s.

By the late 70s, over 60 per cent of G Plan's core customers were aged 45 years or older. The company's conservative style and reasonable, but not cheap, prices meant that their customer base was more likely to be older couples than people furnishing their first homes. Ironically, by the mid-90s, when I was at university, G Plan was so out of favour that people simply threw their items away. Often you could wander the streets and come back

Refinishing G Plan

Use a light sandpaper to sand by hand, avoid mechanical sanding as you don't always realize how deep into the veneer you are going. It will take longer, but you stand a much better chance of not ruining the furniture. Finish with a good-quality teak oil and buff to a shine. Dispose oil-soaked cloths carefully as these are very flammable and should not be left indoors once used. If you damage the veneer or buy a piece cheaply due to damage then repurpose with clever painting techniques or decorative vinyl.

with a nest of tables. I now wince that I once used a set of 'Quadrille' tables as garden furniture, it was so common and thought so little of. Teak furniture was omnipresent at this time in student digs – out of favour cast-offs destined to languish under cheap bottles of 20/20 or Thunderbird and littered with cigarette papers. As they say, 'one man's trash is another's treasure', and at this time retro music and style were in fashion; the term 'mid-century' was in its infancy. I started taking a greater interest in 60s and 70s furniture and furnishing my first home with cast offs from my friends' parents – they thought I was crazy! With the increase in popularity of mid-century style over the past 30 years, G Plan is now highly desirable, along with its contemporaries: Nathan, McIntosh, Beaver and Tapley. People put their own spin on these readily available classics by painting them or placing them on hairpin legs.

Red Label G Plan

Found on furniture from the mid-60s to 1976, and up until the 80s on printed materials like advertising. This label was replaced by the gold label until the mid-80s, which gives a basic insight into the age of the piece you are looking at.

HEAL'S

My inclusion of the Heal's brand within these pages isn't so much to do with the long and illustrious history the brand has within the world of interiors, but for me, more for the impact they made during the 60s and 70s with the fabric that they produced. Fabric and surface print design has always interested and inspired me, and it is still an area that I love to collect from and study. I mostly buy what I find visually appealing with the designer secondary in my mind. A lot of the fabric that I have collected and displayed over the last decade happens to come from Heal's.

Heal's is a company which dates back more than 200 years, known for promoting modern design and employing talented young designers. Its flagship store has been on Tottenham Court Road in London since 1818, at its present location since 1840, and is a mecca for designers. By the end of the nineteenth century, Heal's was the best-known furniture supplier in London. They stopped manufacturing during the Second World War to concentrate on making parachutes for the Allied forces. This enabled them to develop pioneering techniques in textile production and, post-war, they attracted iconic mid-century designers including Lucienne Day, who produced prints for their emerging fabric department, and created over 70 designs for them over a 20-year period.

Heal's was unique in that it didn't have an in-house design department for fabrics. Tom Worthington OBE, joined the company in 1929 and became design director of a subsidiary, Heal's Fabrics, in 1948. The company specialized in selling modern, well-designed printed cottons and dominated the market during the 60s and 70s. Heal's encouraged young designers and favoured progressive designs. Worthington and his assistant Jenni Allen selected around 80 designs a year from over 12,000 submissions. He was responsible for headhunting many of the most successful designers, and employing them while they were still at art college.

One of the golden girls of Heal's Fabrics was Barbara Brown. Born in Manchester, Brown was a Royal College of Art graduate who was famously talent-spotted by Heal's as a student. She produced fabrics for the company throughout the 60s and 70s, and her unusual and instantly recognizable designs are some of the most striking of the twentieth century. She garnered three awards from the Council of Industrial Design between 1968 and 1970. Based on mathematical formulas with a three-dimensional quality, her work is highly collectable and is rising in value as more and more people discover her work, following her first solo exhibition in 2017 at The Whitworth, Manchester. Brown went on to create designs for tableware for Midwinter Pottery, including the 60s design 'Focus'. She also taught at various art colleges including Hornsey, Guildford and Medway, Rochester, where British designer Zandra Rhodes was one of her students.

One of my favourite pieces of fabric from Heal's, and one that influenced and inspired the colour scheme for our dining room is the large stretched canvas entitled 'Cascade' (1972) by Evelyn Redgrave. Little is known about many of the designers who worked for Heal's, despite extensive research, but Redgrave, as with Brown, was also headhunted by Worthington while a student at Hornsey. She worked for Heal's for over seven years, holding a directorship within the company within five years, taking over from Jenni Allen. Redgrave left Heal's and set up her own textile company, Tarian Design, in 1977. 'Cascade', gifted to me by a friend many years ago, remains one of my most cherished stretched fabrics, which many mistake as a piece of art, and one that I will never tire of.

What is notable about these often detailed designs is that they predate CAD (computer-aided design) and digital printing – no such technology existed. These complex fabrics were drafted by hand and printed from individual silk screens, using a separate screen for each colour.

Below is the stretched canvas with 'Cascade' fabric, which was designed by Evelyn Redgrave. This piece hangs in our dining room and was the inspiration for its colour scheme. See page 147 for tips on how to stretch fabric to create your own statement work of art.

TOP LEFT, HEAL'S STORE ON TOTTENHAM COURT ROAD, LONDON, CIRCA 1979. ABOVE, A WIDE SELECTION OF VINTAGE DESIGNS FROM HEAL'S REPURPOSED INTO CUSHIONS BY DEBBIE FROM BLUE LIZARD TEXTILES. LEFT, HEAL'S GOLDEN GIRL, BARBARA BROWN.

"To understand bad taste
one must have very good taste." JOHN WATERS

ELEMENTS OF THE 70s

Plants and planters

The 70s called, they want their Swiss Cheese plant back!

It's no secret that house plants can really enhance your interiors. Carefully placed, they can disguise gaps and soften a room. From tall plants near windows for privacy to the clever use of planters to divide a room, they can also add warmth, ambience and height to a room, as well as creating dramatic shadows when lit from below. When decorating a home with plants I would recommend using attractive ceramic pots. Plastic pots, even expensive ones, tend to look cheap (and yes, I am aware of the irony that my huge *Monstera* is in an awful plastic pot). Thankfully there are plenty of ceramic pots to be found cheaply in thrift stores and car boot sales. More desirable, brightly coloured versions can be hunted down online. These add to the ambience of the interior and can, when used thoughtfully, enhance the natural beauty of the plant. Companies such as Plant Furniture, manufacture contemporary, statement plant pots, which are new or oversized versions of classic 70s planters, in the original German factories as those from the 70s, using the same techniques and high levels of craftsmanship.

One thing that I would almost insist on is that you use caution when placing any plant pot on a varnished surface, as many a teak top has been damaged from this. I use small cork coasters and placemats to protect the wood. Please also heed caution on some plants whose sap can be dangerous for children and animals. Another popular 70s way to display plants is with a bottle garden, or terrarium. These can be made inexpensively from household objects, but were traditionally made from repurposed glass carboys. Original plastic space-age terrariums are now difficult to come by, but a company called Potifiv has reintroduced miniature versions of this classic design. Plants can be bought relatively inexpensively these days, from independent high-street stores to your local supermarket. Even online stores such as Etsy or eBay sell plants, where you might find some more exotic specimens.

I highly recommend the *House Plant Expert* by Dr D.G Hassayon, which has been in continuous print since the 60s (the illustrations and photos in the earlier editions are glorious) and can be picked up cheaply. Since I am no Dr Hassayon, and struggle to keep some plants alive, the following section is a selection of 'can't-kill-em' plants that grow well indoors, suit the aesthetic and look cool to boot.

Dragon Tree
(*Dracaena marginata*)

As at home in Don Draper's Manhattan apartment from *Mad Men* as in a terraced Manchester house, this sexy plant looks particularly good with a tropical-themed interior or bar.

Size Can grow up to 3 metres (10 feet).
Location Tolerates shady areas; does well in bright light and partial shade, avoid direct sunlight.
Care Repot every two years in the spring when roots begin to outgrow the pot. Summer – water frequently to keep soil moist; winter – water sparingly, don't let the soil dry out.
Looking peaky? Brown leaves could mean too much fertilizer; droopy leaves, too much water. Brown tips could mean it's too dry. If leaves are dropping in winter, it's too cold. Older leaves will turn yellow and drop with age as the plant grows.
Toxic? No.

Devil's Ivy
(*Epipremnum aureum*)

This is a vine plant, its heart-shaped glossy leaves can either be left to trail over shelves and in plant hangers or trained to climb up a moss pole, to give height and drama, or dotted around a room for a jungle look.

Size Can grow up to 12 metres (40 feet) long; nip the ends to reduce growth.
Location Bright indirect light; will also tolerate partial shade.
Care Allow the top 2.5 centimetres (1 inch) of soil to dry out between watering; feed every month in the summer. This plant will helpfully tell you when it needs to be watered as it looks 'sad'; likes to be pot bound.
Looking peaky? Yellow leaves are a result of too much water.
Toxic? Harmful if ingested by animals or children. Wash hands after touching sap to avoid irritation.

Swiss Cheese Plant
(*Monstera deliciosa*)

Monster by name and by nature, this beast will take over your home and your life. It looks amazing against strong wall colours.

Size Dramatic and architectural, this iconic 70s plant will grow up to 9 metres (30 feet) tall (we warned you!).

Location Direct light will scorch the leaves, keep in medium light.

Care Allow soil to dry out between waterings, feed every month in the summer, repot to encourage new growth in the spring. As this plant grows it will need additional support from a moss pole. If the plant gets too large, snip out the top.

Looking peaky? Yellow leaves mean too much water, brown leaves too much dry air or direct sunlight.

Toxic? Harmful if ingested by animals or children.

Umbrella Plant
(*Schefflera* or *Heptapleurum*)

A fancy-looking multi-trunked plant with a dainty flower-like pattern on the leaves.

Size Tall and bushy with attractive leaves, can grow up to 1.8 metres (6 feet).

Location Loves bright, indirect sunlight.

Care Summer – water frequently to keep soil moist, do not overwater; winter – water sparingly, don't let the soil dry out. Feed once a month in the summer, repot every year in the spring.

Looking peaky? Dropping leaves is a result of too much or too little water. Turn every few weeks to encourage straight growth; pinch out the top if it gets too tall. If the bottom leaves are dropping, it's not getting enough light.

Toxic? Harmful if ingested by animals or children. Wash hands after touching sap to avoid irritation.

Mother-In-Law's Tongue
or Variegated Snake Plant
(*Sansevieria trifasciata laurentii*)
Spiky and fierce, this classic mid-century house plant is virtually indestructible.

Size Dramatic and architectural, will grow up to 0.9 metres (3 feet) inside, will grow outside in warmer climates.

Location Partial shade will not kill this plant, it can take some direct light, but prefers bright, indirect light.

Care Allow soil to dry out between watering in the summer, around every 2–3 weeks; every 6–8 weeks in winter. Feed through the spring and summer.

Looking peaky? Looking yellow with leaves falling off is usually caused by overwatering. Throw it in the compost heap and start again.

Toxic? Harmful if ingested by animals or children.

Areca Palm
(*Dypsis lutescens*)
This plant creates a jungle feeling in a room. The leafy fronds soften an area – high drama and luxe; think Big Biba vibes.

Size Can grow up to 2.4 metres (8 feet) tall. Most are sold around the 0.9–1.5 metre (3–5 feet) size which creates impact. They can be bought in smaller sizes.

Location Bright, indirect light.

Care Do not overwater; let the top of the soil become dry between watering.

Looking peaky? Brown tips mean that the air is too dry.

Toxic? No.

Spider Plant
(*Chlorophytum comosum*)

A quintessential 70s plant, its iconic striped leaves and tumbling appearance make it great for hangers and shelves.

Size Will grow to 0.6 metres (2 feet) in width and height indoors, if managed correctly.
Location Does well in bright light or partial shade, but it's best to avoid direct sunlight.
Care Water frequently to keep soil moist, but do not allow the plant to stand in water. Feed once a month in spring and summer. Try to water with rainwater or filtered water. It's easy to propagate and the buds will appear from the main plant. Place in water until roots appear, then plant up.
Looking peaky? Overwatering will cause root rot; underwatering will cause the plant to dry out; to avoid brown tips, use rainwater.
Toxic? No.

Rubber Tree
(*Ficus elastica*)

Fake-looking giant, glossy leaves. Likes to be left alone – don't touch it, or move it, as it might start dropping leaves.

Size Can grow from 0.6 metres (2 feet) to giant, depending on the conditions.
Location Bright light.
Care Water when dry; feed twice a month in summer; repot every few years.
Looking peaky? Leaf dropping is usually caused by too much water, being too cold, or not enough light. Lower leaves will naturally drop off with age.
Toxic? Harmful if ingested by animals or children. Wash hands after touching sap to avoid skin irritation.

Be super with a supergraphic

Why did people start painting huge stripes on their walls in the 70s?

The art of supergraphics can be traced back to one woman: Barbara Stauffacher Solomon, a Swiss-trained American graphic designer who combined strict Swiss principles with the 'California Cool' design aesthetic and worked for such esteemed companies as Saul Bass. Supergraphic wall art was a product of necessity, when Barbara was involved with the Sea Ranch project in 1967 (a planned community in California built to preserve the area's natural beauty) and they ran short of finances to decorate. As Barbara herself says: 'Paint was cheap'. This was the first large-scale use of graphic design in a physical environment, and it showed 'where graphics and architecture met'.

The boldness, exuberance and cheery optimism of these painting techniques sum up the decorating excesses of part of the decade. Crazy stripes, arcs, and rainbows covered every conceivable structure from walls to ceilings, floors and furniture. The idea of painting onto the walls of your home and being able to communicate ideas and personal statements became so popular that in 1974 Canadian designer Ted Butler released a DIY kit which retailed at around £5.75 ($7) so that you too could emulate this style. It provides endless colour combinations and designs to play around with and clear instructions on how to achieve the look, all for the price of paint. For me, supergraphics are a favourite way of injecting colour and pattern into a space – they can draw the eye to a specific area of the room, highlight certain features and disguise others. They can be used to bring a colour scheme together with relative ease, using a few rolls of masking tape and a selection of inexpensive tester pots. They are easy to paint over at a later date and also make it straightforward to choose how far to take the design, from simple circles or lines to a full-on mural.

Many of our own in-house designs take inspiration from early supergraphic principles to make a bold statement in the home with the instant hit of wallpaper or removable vinyl for those that feel their DIY skills are not up to par.

One element of mid-century design which keeps coming back as a topic of discussion online is the conversation pit. For the uninitiated, a conversation pit is essentially a sunken section, built into a living space, sometimes accessed by steps, and maybe with a table or a fire at its centre. The idea of this architectural oddity was to bring people together for entertainment, cocktails, parties, games and, most importantly, conversation.

To many they embody the essence of a 70s home, having been featured heavily on television and film, including the *Dick Van Dyke Show*, various Bond films and sets designed for the cult television show, *Mad Men*. American architect Bruce Goff is often credited as the first person to design a modern conversation pit in 1927, the concept was popularized by celebrated architect Eero Saarinen and designer Alexander Girard through The Miller

House, built in 1957 in Columbus, Indiana, which was said to be inspired by Japanese homes. Sunken living continued to grow in popularity during the 50s and 60s as people rejected the social norms, but the 70s is the decade most associated with this controversial living space, with scenes of families relaxing and playing games, or of glamorous people at parties doing other things of a less wholesome nature.

Conversation pits are unusual in the UK, most suited to sprawling US homes, or European pads, though that's not to say that they don't or didn't exist. The first sunken living space I saw was as a child, when a colleague of my father's was converting a barn. Heavily influenced by Japanese culture and the simplicity of living, he went about digging one out at great expense and time. I was fascinated by this cosy, ready-made play pen in the centre of the room, while others were horrified by its concept. I believe that the subsequent owner filled it in immediately.

Despite decades of dominance in interior architecture the allure and glamour of conversation pits began to wane, but why? There are many theories, but one is their lack of versatility, along with safety issues. The former being that guests seated would have a view only of people's feet above them, unflattering angles for anyone wearing skirts or dresses, and stray food and drink falling on guests from above. There was also the risk when people became imbibed with alcohol, that they took a tumble into said pit, taking out the guests with them. Parents with children and pets were also concerned about potential injury, and so a lot of sunken areas started to be filled in.

As the 80s progressed, family rooms became less focused on conversation and entertaining, and more focused on media. Televisions and computer games became the norm, and as a result the family room changed accordingly. We are left with a sofa facing a large flat-screen television which takes centre stage.

It seems that the obsession with conversation pits isn't set to diminish any time soon though. While we are aware of their limitations and possible dangers, there is something so kitsch and quirky about them that screams mid-century. They conjure up an illusion of glamour and sophistication, the ultimate in party lifestyle interiors.

FOR THOSE THAT LONG FOR THE LOOK OF A CONVERSATION PIT BUT AREN'T ABOUT TO START DIGGING INTO THE FOUNDATIONS OF THEIR HOUSES, CLEVER USE OF MODULAR SOFAS CAN MIMIC THIS COSY PIT EFFECT.

Conversation pits

Vinyl

THE HISTORY OF VINYL

Some may assume that patterned vinyl is new to the marketplace, a recent invention of the past few years, but the history of domestic decorative vinyl goes back much further.

The world's most versatile plastic had a rather accidental beginning. American inventor Waldo Semon stumbled on this new material with fantastic properties early in the 20s, during his search for a synthetic adhesive. PVC (polyvinyl chloride) was made popular in the 50s as a decorative, inexpensive and cheerful method that homemakers of the day could use to cheer up their home at little expense. By the 60s and 70s, vinyl, using its trade name of Fablon (or sticky back plastic if you were a 70s *Blue Peter* viewer as a child) had its heyday.

The surge in post-war enthusiasm for the home, interiors and DIY, as popularized by Barry Bucknell, a former Labour councillor who became the television face of home improvement during the 50s and early 60s, who urged the nation to have a go and 'DO IT YOURSELF'. Our grandparents wouldn't have been aware of upcycling or glow-ups, but could have afforded a roll of vinyl to jazz up their kitchen units, which would have possibly been made pre-war and were already 30 years old. To them this was thrifty economics on how to improve the home for less.

Decorative vinyl initially came in a huge range of plain colours and patterns, from sedate pastels to full-on atomic designs in yellows, reds and blues. However, by the 70s, wood grain had appeared on the market, as had swooping psychedelic swirls – these were all marketed with the idea of improving your surroundings with limited cost and experience in DIY, in a short space of time.

MAKE IT POP

Continuing in this tradition of DIY makeovers, we took our own design, 'Yootha', and reworked it into this unique and versatile medium, embracing the ease of use and the ability to change our kitchen instantly, with minimal outlay and risk. This is particularly useful in rented homes, where anyone can personalize their space without losing their deposit. Say goodbye to boring, unloved furniture and kitchen units, save them from the landfill and say hello to bright and cheerful designs that are easy to peel and stick – perfect for any DIY job.

WEST GERMAN POTTERY

If a type of pottery sums up this era, it would be one named 'Fat Lava', typically from West Germany, before the fall of the Berlin Wall in 1989. Its bright and sometimes clashing colours, textured lava-style glaze and solid form make it instantly recognizable. It's a Marmite collection, loved and collected or loathed and derided in equal measure, but there is no doubt that interest and admiration of this once forgotten pottery is on the rise.

West German pottery from the 60s and 70s is an area of collecting which is easy and fairly inexpensive to get into at an entry level, with examples of plant pots still being available at car boot sales for very little money. However, not all West German pottery is equal, and a lot of people are catching onto this area and believing that anything marked W. Germany is desirable and worth a fortune.

The roots of this style of pottery go back to the Bauhaus school of design, but it was not included when the school moved to Dessau in 1925. The post-Second World War boom in industry allowed potteries to invest in workforces and equipment to mass-produce pottery and to experiment with form, glazes and patterns. As a result they produced some of the most stunning and bizarre pottery of the twentieth century.

The production method was industrialized with the use of decorative moulds and slip (liquid clay). Once dry, the glazes were applied by hand, with the firing process activating them and allowing them to erupt into volcanic lava-like life.

The hand-applied glaze means many items are completely unique, despite the use of production moulds. Although popular shapes often didn't change, colour glazes did, from the pastels of the 50s to the oranges, reds and browns of the 60s, to the bright oranges and reds with vibrant purples and eye-popping yellows of the 70s. Most of the potteries are now defunct, with many shutting their doors between the 80s and early 00s. A few, however, are still producing ceramics today, including Otto Keramik (who bought Ruscha Design), Jopeko and Scheurich. Little is known about the individual potteries, with records being destroyed, but many enthusiasts such as Mark Hill and Dr Graham Cooley have dedicated their lives to finding out more about their hobby, with more information coming to light about pottery names and designs all the time.

The most desirable pieces are in bright colours with unusual forms and with the uniquely identifiable bubble 'lava' glaze. Larger floor pottery and lighting tend to be more desirable than smaller pots and vases, with browns and sludge colours least desirable of all. Most pieces can be easily spotted from their glazes and form from a distance, with confirmation of the origin usually marked on the base with 'W. Germany' and a number. Some items will even have their original gilded factory sticker present which will help with identification. Some items were mass-produced, so prices will reflect this; they are, however, still very decorative items to use and enjoy as the manufacturer intended.

Ceramics

A SMALL SELECTION OF WEST GERMAN POTTERY COLLECTED OVER THE YEARS. THESE MASS-PRODUCED VESSELS ARE WIDELY AVAILABLE AND USUALLY AT FAIRLY INEXPENSIVE PRICES. GROUPED TOGETHER ON SIDEBOARDS OR ON SHELVING THEY MAKE AN ATTRACTIVE DISPLAY, ADDING TEXTURE AND INTEREST TO YOUR INTERIOR.

COLOURS, TEXTURES AND MOULDED DESIGN FEATURES ARE
STRONG IDENTIFIERS OF WEST GERMAN POTTERY AT A GLANCE,
AND THIS CAN BE CONFIRMED BY LOOKING ON THE BASE FOR
PATTERN NUMBERS. SOME PEOPLE COLLECT ONE SHAPE IN MANY
DESIGNS, OTHERS COLLECT ONE MAKER. I COLLECT FOR THEIR
INTENDED USE TO DECORATE AND ENHANCE MY INTERIORS.
THE POTS ARE STILL AFFORDABLE SECOND-HAND AND PROVIDE
INTEREST FOR YOUR PLANT COLLECTION.

Look out for the base marked with 'W. Germany' and a number.

What to look for:
* **Bright colours** are more desirable.
* **Lava glaze**
* **Lamps** with cut-out sections and handles with lava glaze.
* **Floor vases** – the bigger and more intricate glazes and colours, the better.
* **Chips and cracks** reduce the value considerably.

HORNSEA

Hornsea designs are instantly recognizable and most of you will have seen at least one piece at some point in your life.

Hornsea Pottery began way back in 1949, a true cottage industry because it started in a cottage where two men made models in plaster of Paris to sell to tourists visiting their seaside town of Hornsea in Yorkshire's East Riding. It wasn't until John Clappison, son of one of the investors, began to get involved in 1958 that things really started to take off. Clappison's work has sold in the millions, with one of his most recognizable designs being the 'Heirloom' design which was released in 1967 and which continued to be sold throughout the 70s. Later came the 'Saffron' and 'Bronte' ranges which were also incredibly popular. By 1974, Hornsea Pottery was turning out over three million pieces per year and was struggling to keep up with demand, so department stores had to be issued with limited quotas. The company had moved to a new factory in Lancaster that same year and received Design Centre Awards which further enhanced their global reputation.

Clappison had left Hornsea in 1972 and became chief designer at Ravenhead Glass in Lancashire. He is the designer responsible for refining and developing the iconic bark design in the 'Siesta' range, originally conceived by Hardie Williamson. He also designed the 'White Fire', 'Icelandic' and 'Topaz' ranges among others, which became popular wedding gifts of the time. He later returned to Hornsea in 1976, until the company went into receivership in 1984 due to the economic downturn. The company was bought out and continued to produce tableware until 2000, when its remaining assets were sold.

Pieces of Hornsea pottery are kept at the V&A Museum, and there is also a dedicated museum in Hornsea itself documenting the history of the company. Collecting Hornsea is incredibly easy, with so many pieces sold originally, it often appears at car boot sales and thrift shops, especially the 'Heirloom' designs, for very little money. It is fairly easy to collect a full service of useful items from various sources quickly and cheaply. There are earlier pieces which fetch considerably more and rarer pieces such as the bird ashtray or the cruet sets which are incredibly desirable.

Because of its availability and low cost, these pots can be easily repurposed into plant pots for indoor plants.

CERAMIC ANIMALS

To be perfectly honest, I'm not sure when ceramic leopards and tigers came into interiors. People have made sculptures of animals for thousands of years and decorated their interiors and tombs with them, but for some strange reason ceramic animals were a thing in the 70s and 80s, and there are many images of them online pictured with stars such as singer Diana Ross.

Over the last few years there has been a notable increase in the interest in 'porcelain pets' – leopards, tigers, panthers, and flamingos have all become desirable in home settings. They have lost their kitsch Liberace appeal and are being seen as de rigueur in even the most tasteful of interiors. I have several in our home, some are vintage, original pieces from the 70s, and some are made from vintage moulds.

I first remember being mesmerized by a pot tiger when I was visiting the home of my mother's boss in the 80s. He had one in his living room, and my mum still refers to it as a monstrosity, but I was enthralled by it. I still love the whimsical and kitsch nature that they bring to a home, and they are one of the things that people don't notice immediately but once they do, they are obsessed with them.

Italian companies have specialized in making these majolica marvels since the 60s and continue to make them in the same time-honoured ways, casting the ceramic slipware and painting them individually by hand, which makes them all unique. Companies such as Dogwood Lifestyle have painstakingly researched their history and work with original suppliers and moulds to bring these vintage beauties back into homes across the world.

Leopards and leopard print have had a mixed past, from glamorous must-have in the pre-war period, when an ocelot coat was the ultimate sign of wealth, to fake fur-wearing caricatures of barmaids with questionable morals portrayed on television in the 70s. They are now more acceptable as a fun and playful interior choice, so much so that leopard print is considered by some as a neutral, as it indeed goes with everything.

Why don't you walk on the wild side and add some big cats to your interior?

Glass

Vintage glass dotted around the home also lends itself to a retro interior. Collecting glass is a very specialist area due to the many varied designs available, as well as the huge number of copies and modern retro-styled pieces on the market, especially from stores such as TK Maxx.

There are many sources of bright-coloured art glass. For anyone wishing to specialize in collecting original pieces from certain designers or factories to complete a look, a little research is required. There are lots of resources online that offer advice on what to look for when purchasing vintage glass and how to avoid getting duped.

Buying from specialist dealers will ensure that something is original and has a provenance. This is important for anyone considering an

investment purchase of a sizeable value. For those who want glass for purely decorative purposes, buy what appeals, and look out for chips and cracks which will detract from any value there is.

Collecting certain styles or colours can be fun and an inexpensive way to accessorize a home. There is usually a plethora of coloured glass available when thrifting, and buying rainbow colours of different shapes and sizes is a charming way to decorate a sunny windowsill. Our own collection of different-coloured bud vases on our windowsill have been purchased for no more than a couple of pounds each, and their varying colours and scales make an interesting collection.

There are, of course, brand names to look out for, which are more desirable and will increase in value over time...

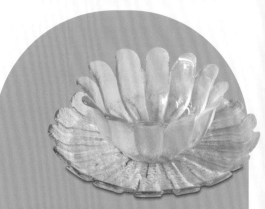

WHITEFRIARS

Known for its high level of quality and creativity, Whitefriars sold in high-class establishments such as Heal's and Fortnum & Mason. Collectors will know the name Geoffrey Baxter, who was one of the most outstanding British glass designers of the post-war period. He was employed by the company from 1954 until its closure in 1980, designing everything from tableware to ornamental glass. He is best known for his unusual shapes and bright pops of colour.

Much of the success of Baxter's designs reflects the switch from traditional lead crystal to soda glass, which was cheaper and more flexible to work with. This, along with the bright and almost psychedelic colours that he helped introduce, such as tangerine orange and aubergine, ruby and kingfisher blue, were key. His most recognized works were introduced in the latter part of the 60s and early 70s; he was influenced greatly by nature and used nails, copper wire and even tree bark to imprint unusual textures into the glass moulds. These were a huge success, meeting the demand for affordable, yet modern design.

The value of Baxter's work boils down to colour: with cinnamon classed as the least desirable and tangerine the most common. Rarer shades such as willow, kingfisher or indigo will fetch higher prices in the same shapes; the highest valued colours are meadow green, aubergine and ruby red.

DARTINGTON GLASS

Staff at Dartington were trained by 16 glassblowers from Swedish glass manufacturers Kosta and Orrefors under the design direction of co-director and chief designer Frank Thrower. His vision was to produce clean and simple designs, handmade using age-old Scandinavian techniques, and he made over 700 popular and innovative designs during his prolific 20-year tenure, until his early death in 1987. A self-taught, self-made man who began as a salesman, Thrower provided the creative and marketing knowledge that buoyed the company's success. Popular designs are his flower and Greek key design vases, stark hexagonal designs and the famous range of 'Daisyware', which included everything from platters to trifle dishes and vases.

The 'Sharon' Collection designed by Thrower was included in the '100 Best Ever Products' exhibition at the Victoria and Albert Museum in London. Designed in 1971, this modern classic set of wine glasses, which are suitable for all wine types, and feature an elegant stem with an individual mouth-blown teardrop. Both the 'Sharon' and 'Daisy' range are available through their website, with the 'Daisy' being reintroduced through popular demand. Dartington Crystal, as it is now known, is an award-winning visitor attraction in Devon, which produces over 1,400 pieces a day.

ITALIAN GLASS

The pieces of glassware I most associate with the 70s are Italian decanters, traditionally made in Tuscany in, or around the Empoli region. My grandparents had them sitting on the window, glinting in the light, and they fascinated me. These bottles that either housed bubble bath, wine or were for simple decorative pleasure are commonly described as 'genie' bottles. They were made very crudely, designed for tourists as cheap souvenirs, but they have become highly collectable in recent years.

The most popular and traditional colour for these bottles is verde (green), a direct result of the make up of the local sand which is used to produce the glass. They often have 'Empoli' or 'Made in Italy' in raised letters on the bottom.

I have bought and sold many of these in my time, and at one point I was overrun with them, having paid no more than a few pounds each. Designs include straight sides, flat, squat bottoms, swirls, bubbles, moons and stars (which my grandparents had) and a 'hobnail' effect. They are often found without their stoppers at the top which are easily broken. Most common are the greens, followed by the blues and ambers. Rarer colours such as reds and pinks are the most desirable which often fetch large sums of money, especially in Australia where there is high demand for them.

MURANO

The history of glassmaking in Venice goes as far back as the thirteenth century and, after concerns about fire risks, with the mainly wooden structures of Venice, works were moved to the offshore island of Murano. Common pieces are usually figurative, such as animals or clowns in bright, lurid colours. Mottled fish were popular during the 50s and 60s, found swimming in schools across teak furniture – these are now firmly rooted in kitsch folklore. More desirable pieces, which are stunning in their simplicity, include cased single-colour lightshades, bark-textured discs and tubes suspended from vast chandeliers, which create a truly breathtaking statement light.

Venini has been creating statement glassware in this style since 1921, working with designers such as Ettore Sottsass (who designed the sexiest mirror known to man: the Ultrafragola Poltronova). Through the 70s Venini produced lighting which can still be seen today in luxury hotels such as the Mandarin in Singapore; in the Moulin Rouge in Paris, and the Schloss Theatre in Schwetzingen, Germany. It even produced statement lights for the rebuilt World Trade Center. Other Murano pieces experiencing a revival are the mushroom-shaped glass lamps which became popular in the 70s. Their simple, organic shape combined with pastel colours and a signature wave design are highly desirable and collectable today.

Space age

Space-age design was influenced by the atomic age, from the splitting of the atom in the 30s to the development of nuclear weapons and the Cold War up until the early 60s. Atomic design is encompassed in mid-century design, and includes Googie architecture from Southern California. Inspiration came from iconography of atoms, resulting in the boomerang shape, used primarily in tables and surface prints; wire or narrow, tapered legs; and brightly coloured balls and star bursts. Space-age design started gaining popularity during the mid-50s, spanning not only furniture, but architecture, automotive and clothes by the mid-60s. Fashion designers such as André Courrèges and his 1964 spring collection showcased linear minidresses with cut-out panels, and astronaut-inspired accessories such as helmets and goggles, which summed up the futuristic appeal in design. Off the catwalk, some of the period's most iconic designs were in the home. Although designed at least a decade earlier, they retained popularity until the mid- to late 70s. Classic pieces such as the 'Tulip' chair or 'Pedestal' table, arguably the most recognized of Eero Saarinen's designs, were developed in 1956. Tables, chairs and stools with a delicately curved pedestal fluting into a circular base, inspired later designs in the 60s and 70s by Arkana and Hille. This iconic design was featured in Stanley Kubrick's *2001: A Space Odyssey*. Released in 1968, the film was a commercial flop until it was re-released in 1971, further cementing space-age design into the cultural idiom of the 70s.

Eero Aarnio is a Finnish interior designer famous for his futuristic, plastic and fibreglass chairs, which featured heavily in science-fiction sets. They were perfect in their simplicity, notably the 'Bubble' chair, a clear suspended sphere, and the 'Ball' chair, which featured heavily in the cult television series *The Prisoner*. This almost certainly inspired Danish designer Henrik Thor-Larsen's 'Ovalia' chair, designed in 1968, but which sold right up until 1978, and featured in the 1997 film

Keracolor television

Weltron 2005 hi-fi

'Panton' chair

Men In Black, and also the early 70s Panasonic 'Audio Egg', which took a fibreglass egg chair and wired it for sound. Another design classic which has spawned many replicas is the 'Panton' chair or 'S-Chair' by another Danish designer, Verner Panton, who created many innovative and futuristic designs, working with a variety of materials. He is especially known for his futuristic designs in vibrant coloured plastics. One such example is his 'S-Chair Model 275', manufactured by Thonet in 1965, which was the world's first cantilevered plywood chair. A later version followed, Model 276, which was made from moulded plastic and sold from 1967 onwards, and continues to be manufactured by Vitra. Modern colours such as vibrant yellows, warm oranges, bright reds and electric blues were teamed with stark monochrome white and black to give a truly striking and futuristic look.

Sleek in appearance, space-age design with its stark minimalism is timeless and fits as well in modern settings as with vintage pieces. One such success is the 'Componibili' storage unit, designed in 1967 by Anna Castelli Ferrieri, an Italian architect and designer for her husband's company, Kartell. Designed to be functional yet simply beautiful, this unit can be stacked at different heights without being bolted together and is light enough to be moved about easily. It's still one of Kartell's best-selling pieces and is in production today.

My nod to space-age is the 1970 Keracolor television in the living room, designed in Cheshire by inventor Arthur Bracegirdle, along with engineer Howard Taylor. The set originally sold for £375 ($400) in Harrods which would be over £6,000 ($7,300) today. Keracolor also made a hanging model, but more well-known is the 'Videosphere', a black and white television, launched in 1970 by Japanese company JVC, produced in white, black, red and orange plastic shells. Other fun pieces include Panasonic's range of personal radios such as the R-70 'Panapet'. They also made the 'Toot-a-Loop' R-72 radio, designed to be wrapped around a wrist. The holy grail of space-age stereos is the 'Weltron 2001', released in 1970–71, which was the first portable 'boom box' to contain both eight-track and AM/FM radio. Better still is the much admired 'Weltron 2005', released in 1973, which had an integrated radio and eight-track, and model 2007, released in 1975, which was a record player with integrated AM/FM audio receiver and a compact cassette recorder. Both of these vinyl players feature a UFO spherical unit with domed plexiglass top. Complement it with the S-45 fluted tulip shape stand, à la Eero Saarinen's 'Pedestal' collection.

HOW I CREATED THE SPACE-AGE STUDY

Early 70s space-age furniture is very desirable and therefore difficult to find on a budget. I wanted something that was clean and streamlined and reminiscent of the Drexel or Broyhill units found in the US. Second-hand IKEA units were purchased and upcycled with plain, bright vinyl to give this effect. Upcycled Ladderax units, purchased for £20 ($25) from Facebook Marketplace, were fitted in the chimney breast alcoves and vinyl supergraphics were applied to the bright, white walls. Yellow shagpile was added to the floor and vintage accessories were used. The Eero Saarinen's 'Tulip' Carver chair has been teamed with a repurposed 'Docksta' table from IKEA via Facebook Marketplace and a custom desk top was also applied.

Mass-market art

What is mass-market art?

Between the 50s and 80s, high-street shops like the dearly departed Woolworth's and the well-known chemist Boot's sold large numbers of commercially produced art, most of which were colourful and sentimental pieces. These artworks are well recognized, with many people's grandparents, aunties or parents having at least one hanging in their family home. These iconic and often kitsch works were mocked for their naivety, poor execution and dubious taste; however, this did not stop them being bought in their thousands and displayed proudly in homes. Even Biba, the most beautiful store in the world, got in on the action selling mass-market art in its kitsch room.

These pictures are the forerunners of the late-70s trend for mass-produced Athena posters to be mounted and displayed in homes. Some of the earlier examples are from Russian-born South African artist Vladimir Tretchikoff, known as 'the king of kitsch', who painted the iconic *Chinese Girl* (often referred to as the *Green Lady*) in 1952, which went on to become one of the bestselling works of the twentieth century. This postmodern classic is still as enigmatic and popular across the world today. It is equally at home on the cover of an interiors magazine or above the mantelpiece in a working-class terrace home. Prints of this image can be seen in *Frenzy*, the 1972 film by Alfred Hitchcock, and also a moustachioed version in the sketch show, *Monty Python's Flying Circus*. The original painting of *Chinese Girl*, featuring the model Monika Pon-su-san, was sold in 2013 at Bonhams, London and fetched a hammer price of nearly £1 million ($1,155,805 in 2013). Over the years, critics have tried to dismiss Tretchikoff's work as 'token art' to which he gleefully would reply: 'Art can reach the heart, but kitsch can make you rich.' It was noted that after Picasso, he was the richest artist of the twentieth century. Tretchikoff was often quoted as saying: 'I don't do portraits'. To him, 'his ladies' were a product of a woman in the street, or a model, but mostly from the riches of his imagination. He always referred to his artwork as 'symbolic realism'. He is also known for works such as *Balinese Girl*, 1959; *Miss Wong* 1952–53; *Lady of the Orient*,

Care for your mass-market art

* I have bought items at car boot sales which have been filthy and covered in nicotine. This is easy to deal with when the frame is solid and the picture is glazed since you can easily wipe the picture clean, but it becomes more problematic when the picture is directly on the board. I have on occasion had some success with gently wiping the print with a wet wipe. This will get most of the grime off, but please do this with caution and test in an inconspicuous area before tackling the entire print.

* Do not allow the print to get wet as it will delaminate from the original board.

* Always keep your print out of direct sunlight – sun will fade the art, quicker if unglazed and you will be left with a less than attractive green/blue hue all over the image.

* Regular dusting will keep the picture clean.

1953; and still life of flowers such as *Lost Orchid* as well as his paintings of animals such as *Mother and Child*.

Another ubiquitous artwork is by British artist Joseph Henry Lynch: *Tina*, a sultry, tree-hugging siren with luscious locks and smouldering eyes (opposite, top). *Tina* and her somewhat lesser well-known sisterhood of *Autumn Leaves*, *Rose* and various nymphs, not only seductively graced the walls of aspirational homes, but can be seen on the walls of Alex's parents' home in the 1971 Stanley Kubrick film *A Clockwork Orange*. For an artist whose work has entered the cultural psyche of more than a generation, little is known about J. H. Lynch. So little, in fact, that there is almost no information regarding who he was, other than that he was a British commercial artist who sadly passed away in 1989 without note for the impact he had on twentieth-century art and the lives of ordinary people.

We cannot discuss mass-market art and the 70s without touching on the classic *Wings of Love* (see page 70) by Stephen Pearson. This surrealist, kitsch masterpiece which is quasi-religious and quasi-pornographic depicts a naked couple against a backdrop of a swan; highly romantic as swans apparently mate for life. By the early 90s, over 2.5 million copies had been recorded as being sold, which makes it one of the most popular prints sold in history. Not only has this print gone down in history as the archetypal kitsch 70s painting, but it was immortalized in Mike Leigh's 1977 play *Abigail's Party* (see page 170), a situational comedy and satire on the new middle class that emerged in Britain in the 70s. Beverly Moss, played both on stage and screen by Alison Steadman, proudly produces the painting, much to the disgust of her husband Laurence.

Two artists, whose works were originally aimed at a more middle-class customer, were Leonard Pearman and David Shepherd CBE who famously painted wildlife, such as tigers prowling through the undergrowth, which can be seen in our own home, and of majestic elephants thundering across plains. By the 80s these were typecast as being dated and of low-brow taste, often depicted against the famous bamboo wallpaper in the Trotters' flat in the BBC comedy series *Only Fools and Horses*. Along with 50s larder units, 60s cocktail bars and loud and proud 70s curtains, this illustrates how, by the early 80s the everyday tastes of the average householder of the 70s were starting to be mocked for comedic effect.

> "Just because a picture happens to be erotic does not make it pornographic."
> **Beverly Moss –**
> *Abigail's Party*

What to look for

Often iconic images of the period are heavily reproduced. There are good and mediocre copies available, which means that you can get the look for less, but what if you desire an original print from the 60s or 70s? Reputable vintage dealers will be able to advise you so that you are not paying a premium for a modern reproduction, but some key aspects to look out for when buying mass-market art in the wild are as follows:

✴ **Frame** – most frames were either a simple, plain white moulding or one with a raised gold tone relief. This delicate plaster effect may have become chipped over the years which would indicate an older piece. If it looks and feels right, then most likely it is. A brand-new frame would ring alarm bells.

✴ **Glazing** – a few examples were glazed; a lot were printed directly onto the board which obviously wouldn't fare so well after 50-plus years. Glazed examples will always command more money. There is nothing wrong with unglazed versions.

✴ **Labels** – always check the back of the print; some prints bear the name of the artist and subject on the back of the picture and the place where they were purchased. These occasionally fall off over the years, but an example with an original sticker will always be a reassuring sign.

✴ **Backing** – most of the prints are held in with brown tape and pins rather than staples.

✴ **Print quality** – watch out for paying a high price for a scratched, faded or water damaged piece. If buying online, study the image closely to look for these defects.

Kitsch

I first heard this word used in the context of my own work when I was 15, in life drawing class when I decided not to use flesh tones for the model but a bold combination of greens, yellows, blues, oranges and reds. The precise origins of the word is unknown but it is believed to be a derivation of the German slang *etwas verkitschen*, meaning to 'make cheap' or *kitschen* – 'to collect junk from the street'. Often historically used by upper and middle classes to dismiss the mass-market and banal tastes of the working class, kitsch has almost always been about people with presumed superiority over the stylings of popular culture.

To brand something as kitsch was once derogatory, but now can also be defined as an ironic 'so bad it is good' style choice and represent a form of inverted snobbery. Modern kitsch started post-war when, for the first time, working-class people had disposable income to spend on cars and holidays, furniture and accessories. Above all, after years of austerity, they wanted colour and fun! The 70s has been dubbed the ultimate decade of kitsch – a come-down from the drug-induced swinging 60s psychedelic movement, straight into glam rock, through disco and taking a left turn at anarchic punk.

Collecting kitsch items is also a form of escapism. It's partly nostalgic, for items held dear in my own youth, or items I was denied in my youth. Venezuelan historian Celeste Olalquiaga sums it up perfectly in her book *The Artificial Kingdom*: 'Kitsch is the world as we would like it to be; not as it is... kitsch is a flight from the present... an enchanted grotto.' I think as a nation, the UK has an inbuilt appreciation for kitsch. Part of the reason I love it is because it is divisive and items like concrete garden statues in the shape of toads, gnomes, flamingos and fairy lights make me smile. They make my heart sing and make me take life a little less seriously.

What iconic items are considered kitsch when it comes to interiors? The list is extensive, but here are a few of my favourites...

COCKTAILS

Are cocktails kitsch? I think so. First off the bat is the array of ephemera that goes with them, from bright, colourful glasses and hula girl cocktail shakers to boat-shaped bars, crazy coloured swirlers and of course the ubiquitous cocktail umbrella with a lurid red and syrupy almond-flavoured maraschino cherry. The names of the cocktails themselves can also be classed as kitsch and possibly cringy. Cute names such as Pink Squirrel or Grasshopper, but also more sexually liberated ones including Sex on the Beach and Slippery Nipple. Want to know more about cocktails? Head on over to our entertaining section on page 166 to find out more.

GARDEN GNOMES

Originating in Germany and imported to England in 1850 by Sir Charles Isham, the original gnome still resides at the family seat of Lamport Hall, Northamptonshire and is valued at more than £1 million ($1,155,805). Having polled my followers, it's pretty much a 50:50 split of people either loving them or loathing gnomes. I have them dotted around the garden; they are so ridiculous that it makes me laugh seeing them.

ANIMAL PRINT

Author Lesley Gillian states in *Kitsch Deluxe* that 'Reproducing the coats of endangered jungle predators in tame polyester is the ultimate in frivolous kitsch'. Faux fur leopard and tiger print has long been associated with louche women (and men). Think Bet Lynch from *Coronation Street*. Leopard print is now more acceptable in fashion as well as interiors, and whether you see it as exotic, glamorous, bad taste or kitsch, it has stood the test of time.

NOVELTY LIGHTING

This rain lamp looks like something found in a dubious Italian restaurant circa 1976, but I am a little obsessed with these beauties. Either a table lamp or hanging from a chain, the bulb at the top provides the lighting and a reservoir for mineral oil at the base with a pump. The oil is pumped up the exterior poles and then proceeds to 'rain' down the plastic filament lines which make it look like it is indeed raining. At the centre there is usually a figure, often a Greek or Roman goddess, and then lots of plastic fish tank foliage.

ROYAL FAMILY MEMORABILIA

What is more kitsch than riding around in a gold horse-drawn coach and living in a palace? Memorabilia surrounding the Royals intrigue me. Souvenirs from pivotal events such as coronations, births, weddings and jubilees are a rich source for collecting. Some years ago, I was interested in any giftable 'tat' from the late Queen's Silver Jubilee in 1977, and for the anarchists there is also the Sex Pistols' 'God Save The Queen' of the same year.

BUTLIN'S

This British institution that was once described as a 'cross between Disneyland and an army barracks' lingers long in the memories of childhood nostalgia. Following the war, Billy Butlin started his camps as a cheap, all-inclusive British holiday, featuring beachcomber bars, mock Tudor pubs, fake tropical murals and miles of plastic flowers. Entertainment was provided by the 'Red Coats', an overtly cheerful bunch who organized knobbly knee and glamorous granny competitions. The Butlin's gift shop sold merchandise with logos on, which can often be found at car boot sales and in vintage shops.

FLAMENCO DOLLS

Souvenirs of the Spanish package holiday, along with straw donkeys, sangria bottles covered in rattan, castanets and embroidered postcards, these are the embodiment of kitsch.

FAIRY LIGHTS

The term was first coined in 1881, when British inventor Sir Joseph Swan lit up London's Savoy Hotel with 1,200 incandescent light bulbs. By the 70s Pifco manufactured various shapes of fairy lights such as multicoloured icicles, bells, Victorian lanterns, Cinderella carriages and fibre optic orbs. Fairy or string lights are now perfectly acceptable to use in the garden all year round.

FAKE FRUIT AND FLOWERS

Simply put, recreating nature in plastic lurid colours – the epitome of kitsch.

FLAMINGOS

Lawn flamingos, or 'mingos, are the ultimate in tacky, kitsch garden ornaments. They first came into existence in 1957 when classically trained artist Don Featherstone sculpted the first lawn 'mingo (which he named Diego) for Union Products. Over 20 million of the original Featherstone flamingos have been sold and the design has been copied by many other manufacturers.

MURALS

Island settings, orange sunsets, woodland scenes and mountain ravines, all blown up onto wallpaper so that you can paste it onto your living room wall – if that isn't kitsch, I don't know what is.

PEOPLE

Kitsch isn't just related to items, it can also be used to describe people. A few that fit the bill are: rock 'n' roll king Elvis Presley, with his 70s Vegas-era rhinestone jumpsuits and ostentatious Graceland home, including the jungle room with a backlit waterfall feature; and Mr Showmanship himself, Liberace, the richest piano player in history, famed for his lavish costumes, and lines such as 'Why don't I slip into something more spectacular?' During the 60s and 70s he owned eight homes, all furnished in his unique style of gold, crystal and marble with trademark candelabras – he even had a marble and gold bath tub costing over £46,000 ($55,000). Not to be outdone was Hollywood starlet Jayne Mansfield and her pink palace, with its pink faux fur-covered walls, gold taps and heart-shaped pool; and the queen of kitsch Dolly Parton, who famously said 'I ain't dumb and I ain't blonde', with her taste for larger-than-life bejewelled costumes, decorated denim and big hair. She has also immortalized her version of kitsch in the form of her own theme park: 'Dollywood'.

Colour bathrooms

Over the past two decades, white bathrooms have dominated, making clean, sterile rooms. Coloured bathroom suites were last mass-produced in the early 00s, as they were considered expensive in light of their decline and the changing fashions.

The trend for all things colour started in the 20s in the US. It began as a sales ploy to get people to purchase 'fashion' colours such as primrose yellow, pale pink, jade green and baby blue, and it worked. These colours became the chic alternative to white through the 20s to the 70s and even in 80s homes, with colours such as primrose being in constant manufacture in the UK from 1934 to 1979 and sky blue from 1957 to 1980. Most people colour-coordinated their closed couple toilets with matching tiles and wallpaper and bath sets (bath mat, under the toilet rug and toilet seat cover) – I remember my paternal grandmother sporting a rather lurid purple and lilac furry number in her downstairs loo.

Bathrooms encountered the most transformation during the 70s, from being necessary and functional places to ones of spa relaxation luxury. Not only did they become larger, but more bathrooms were included in modern house designs. If you weren't lucky enough to have an en suite, vanity units became hugely popular – basically a sink set into a Formica unit,

but in a bedroom. They were available in a huge array of hues to match modern bedroom décor.

Although architects built and designed houses using bold colour schemes with primary colours and contrasting tiles, such as the German ceramics specialist Villeroy & Boch's collaboration with Luigi Colani, the average household was entertaining mid-range bathrooms in new acrylic colours. They favoured larger, inbuilt showers, as opposed to showers over the bath; his and hers basins; concealed plumbing; and wall-to-wall carpets. Although we baulk at the idea of a carpeted bathroom today, back then it was the height of sophistication and luxury. Most modern houses had central heating for the first time and carpets highlighted the dryness and warmth of the bathroom. It was in stark contrast to previous decades where bathrooms were cold, damp and inhospitable places with slippery lino flooring. It also became fashionable to have the bath in the centre of the room on a plinth, or a sunken or even a shaped bath. Corner baths were considered extremely risqué due to the connotations that they weren't for sole occupancy.

Mirror tiles became a stylish option in bathrooms with little natural light, and it was heavily advertised that you could now finish your bathroom to the same standard of luxury as the rest of your home. This was years before the 'greed is good' mentality of the 80s, with 24 carat gold taps, some in fanciful shapes such as swans and dolphins, making an appearance along with onyx and marble features

that became hugely popular.

Brighter-coloured bathroom designs had started to emerge through the late 60s, with pampas green being introduced in 1973, the forerunner to the most famous and ubiquitous of bathroom colours, the much-maligned avocado green suite, which was introduced into suburban homes in 1976 by Twyford. The 70s were a time when the green bathroom reigned supreme, no longer the colour of a fruit but now also a toilet. My own gran introduced one in the late 70s or early 80s, and we were dubious, bearing in mind she had also committed other crimes against interiors and not only laid carpet in the bathroom, but carpeted up the side of the bath. She also had 'best' towels that weren't for use and only for display. Seemingly enough time has passed that this bathroom colour has gone full circle from high fashion, to being mocked and considered a design abomination and ripped out in the 90s and 00s, to now being appreciated as the quintessential colour of the 70s bathroom. For me? I prefer the warmer tones of harvest or sepia, such as the limited-edition silver jubilee toilet with gold trim created by Twyford Bathrooms in 1977.

The interest in all things historic by the end of the decade, along with the start of people buying and renovating period properties, resulted in a keenness for more of a period look with Victorian-styled high-level cisterns and roll-top baths teamed with Laura Ashley and Sanderson prints.

Bolder colours and designs were used by some companies, most notably in 1975 when Villeroy & Boch commissioned German industrial designer Luigi Colani, who was known for his futuristic designs combined with organic shapes to create a bathroom suite. Villeroy & Boch cite that his creations for their brand marked the start of 'transforming bathrooms into a living space'.

HOW I CREATED

A DISCO BATHROOM

While other people renovating a bathroom headed to their local hardware store, I started looking in local skips from house renovations and on online auctions for a coloured suite. I had a jade green Armitage Shanks suite in my last house, and I find it so sad that these historic pieces are ripped out in favour of something so bland and the same as the next person has.

The archetypal 70s avocado bathroom suite was swiftly vetoed by His Nibs (my partner) as 'disgusting', saying 'we had one as kids; I hated it'. One night when browsing eBay, I typed in 'retro bathroom', I saw it, I laughed, scrolled on, then scrolled back...The photos were awful, but as I skipped through to the end, I knew I had to make this work, somehow. Bidding was successful and the suite was ours for a grand total of £20 ($25). Research shows that it is a rare design by Selles Cheverney, a French company that specialized in luxury bathrooms. The colour is called *feuilles d'automne jaspées*, or autumn leaves. It's so rare, in fact, that a replacement seat cost a LOT more than the actual bathroom, such is the way of things.

Getting the bathroom itself is the easy part. Second-hand bathrooms have old fixtures and fittings, often in imperial sizes which don't easily correspond to modern metric plumbing. They also have been in use for many years and sometimes show the signs of age, especially any plastic parts which can become discoloured. I will say that the quality of these pieces is amazing and

that with a little hard work and imagination an old suite can become stunning once more. The key to getting your dream retro bathroom is finding someone mad enough to take the job on. Plumbers are naturally suspicious of old suites, but there are plenty of people out there who love the challenge. If, however, you want the retro look without the knowledge that someone else's bottom has been sitting on that toilet daily for 50 years, then there are companies such as The Bold Bathroom Company who are currently making modern suites in vintage colours. They also have a sister company called Brokenbog, which specializes in reclaimed original bathrooms, ideal if you are missing a piece from a suite.

I initially wanted original 70s tiles but trying to find enough new tiles in the right colour is nigh on impossible; reclaimed are more common but cleaning off grout and adhesive is a laborious task. Thankfully since the renovation there are more companies coming up with tiles that would complement the scheme, due to the current rise in interest in coloured bathrooms. I consulted one of my many source books and saw an image of mosaic tiles in a mirror effect. I knew I wanted something luxury, something that wouldn't look out of place in a boutique hotel, yet screamed 70s, and I complemented this with some ceramic marble-effect tiles.

When designing the bathroom, I knew I wanted some sort of softness to it. I love

the natural look of wood and the appeal of mid-century wood panelling, so wanted to incorporate this into the design. However, working with the luxury and glamour of the overall aesthetic, I didn't simply want wood tongue and groove, I wanted something FABULOUS. I've always loved the architecture of London's Royal Festival Hall with its teak-clad modernist interiors as well as the 70s trend for wood cladding, especially in US houses. I decided on a faux acoustic wood design in a warm brown to complement the bathroom suite. I teamed this with an acid-etched copper radiator to blend in with the surroundings rather than a towel rail due to the size constraints of the tiny room. As the room is so small, I wanted to give the illusion of space. I decided to team the mirrored tiles I selected with an uber 70s smoked-glass mirror on the opposite wall to reflect the light in what is a darkly decorated north-facing room. Of course, I cannot afford a real smoked-glass mirror, so I used mirror acrylic. This is a brilliant, cost-effective and style-conscious alternative to glass,with the added benefits of being safe, light and durable.

I knew that I wanted to continue the warm and luxe 70s vibe through to the ceiling, so I painted it gold. Ceilings are often overlooked and left white, but I felt that this was too stark in comparison to the rest of the design. I have also continued this paint onto the door and architrave to unify and give a cohesive finish. I also painted the existing UPVC window with spray primer and paint; it took a couple of hours to carefully mask the window off and spray the coats I needed, but the effect is amazing and with a little patience is a low-cost solution to changing a very expensive item.

The Lan-Bar dolphin range of fittings, original to the 70s, gives a real luxurious,

Hollywood regency feel to the bathroom. I find that by sourcing vintage pieces, it really gives an air of authenticity, not to mention cost effectiveness. I would never be able to purchase 24-carat gold fittings without hunting them down at car boot sales and auctions.

The amazing original smoked glass mirror above the toilet was also an eBay find for £20 ($25) – a complete bargain. I love the internal line decoration which reminds me of paintwork from custom cars of the era. As with all vintage pieces, this isn't perfect, the mirror itself has a bit of foxing on the glass, but this doesn't bother me. I love that these pieces have stood the test of time and they are usually better made and better quality than pieces made today. I styled the bathroom with plants, both real and faux, which helped to pull the scheme together, allowing the room to look more lived in and less sterile. The *Kentia* palms were perfect for the vibe I was going for, which was pure 70s Biba meets Studio 54 with an air of Hollywood glamour.

Bathrooms are an expensive purchase and often the suite can cost £1,000 ($1,153). I have made significant cost cuts by sourcing most things either second-hand at a greatly reduced rate, or through discount options and clever design solutions. I hope that I have shown you that a second-hand bathroom suite can once again look as if it belongs in Studio 54.

Kitchens

Before the invention of fitted kitchens, rooms were organized with freestanding elements such as dresser units, sinks and some appliances. This made the space chaotic, inefficient and unhygienic to clean. Fitted kitchens were originally pioneered in the US, but not adopted in the UK until well into the post-war period. Streamlined, coordinated units with built-in appliances and a continuous worktop really came into their own in the 70s. Many brands offered sleek units, breakfast bars, island units and all the modern conviveences such as built-in ovens, dishwashers and microwaves, the latter being made available to domestic customers for the first time in the UK in 1974. This drive towards labour-saving devices and easy maintenance dominated the latter part of the twentieth century and continues in much the same way today.

If you opt for a fitted kitchen today, one thing that stands out with off-the-peg units is the lack of colour, unless you go bespoke, which is very expensive. Modern, sterile kitchens, much like bathrooms, aren't much to write home about, but, not so long ago, kitchens were bright and bold. It started quietly in the 60s, but by the 70s they were a riot of colour that has not been seen since. Colour had always been popular in kitchens, especially in the US, since the 50s. By the 60s wood had replaced metal as the unit of choice, but by the 70s laminated coated chipboard had become incredibly popular with wipe-clean laminated worktops. While the majority of kitchens in design magazines and books of the period do not reflect those of the typical household, there is an insight into what the average family were purchasing, which can be seen while flicking through adverts in household magazines of the period.

Companies such as Hygena, Schreiber and Wrighton introduced 'fully metric kitchens' (the UK didn't go metric until the late 70s, and some may argue that it has never gone fully metric). These were available in bright, bold colours offset by brilliant white and were marketed as the latest in luxury. The kitchen manufacturers often worked in partnership with companies such as Creda and Kenwood to supply ovens and hobs, and Manchester-based Pilkington for tiles.

During the decade, open-plan living started to become more popular, with kitchens becoming the hub of the house, central to raising a family and entertaining. With the rise in home ownership and home improvements, the small kitchen, having been previously separated from the rest of the house, now incorporated a dining area and possibly even a living area.

FAR LEFT, THE HOME OF DAVID FROM @THE_AVOCADO_LAIR. LEFT, KITCHENS OF THE 70S WERE CHEERFUL, BRIGHT AND COLOURFUL, OFTEN USING POPS OF SATURATED COLOUR AND HEAVILY PATTERNED TILES ALONG WITH PURE WHITE AS A CLEAN BASE.

By the late 70s, the farmhouse-style kitchen became fashionable, with an urge to shun the space-age simplicity of the 60s and early 70s and return to the bucolic charm of rural Victoriana. This was in no doubt influenced by the rise in popularity of fashion designers such as Laura Ashley who popularized this quaint farmhouse style though her clothing, and later interiors, well into the 80s.

This is exactly what happened in our home when I was growing up. My parents inherited a yellow and white Hygena kitchen, which has heavily influenced my own kitchen inspiration, and they modernized it by replacing the cabinet doors with wooden ones in the 80s.

In the decade where convenience food became available, and where people still entertained with dinner parties, oven to tableware became increasingly popular. There were many varieties available; one popular design was Denby 'Arabesque' (also known as 'Samarkand' in the US), designed by Gill Pemberton. It has a striking, bold 70s design with yellows and oranges on a brown background with white satin glaze insides, which were all hand painted until the mid-70s. Although mass produced, this design continues to be popular with collectors.

Our own oven-to-tableware collection includes Midwinter pieces designed by Jessie Tait (see page 89); 'Flowersong', released in 1972, which is a stylized daisy in mustards and orange with a black outline; and 'Nasturtium', Tait's last design for Midwinter, which is a 1974 design of stylized flowers in reds, oranges, yellows and olive greens. Both designs are in use daily in our home and are dishware-proof and look just as good today as they did 50 years ago. You can find individual plates or complete sets online, or if you are lucky in second-hand shops and at car boot sales.

PYREX

Pyrex glass ovenware has been an essential part of the kitchen since the early twentieth century in the US, and was first marketed in the UK after the First World War. Pyrex can withstand oven temperatures without cracking and reduces cooking times by better use of heat to ensure even cooking. The glass made them an attractive alternative to pots and pans when serving food to guests. From the early 20s James A. Jobling made Pyrex under licence in the UK, and their range included everything a modern home could want, from jugs to mixing bowls, roasting trays, divided dishes and various casserole dishes.

Pyrex is now hugely collectable, mostly due to the nostalgic value of using something that your parents or grandparents used. Prices can vary from a few pounds to thousands, depending on its age, colour and rarity. For example, in 2020, a Gold Constellation 474 mid-century 'Starburst' complete with lid was sold for £4,776 ($5,655).

Care for your vintage Pyrex

* Do not use abrasive pads or cleaners, use warm soapy water.
* Do not put vintage Pyrex in the dishwasher as it will discolour and go cloudy.
* Avoid sudden temperature changes on your Pyrex.
* Do not use on an open flame.

Popular 70s designs include birds, graphic circles and squares. Designs that I connect with most are the designs that I grew up with, including:

* 'Chelsea' 1967–78: This features a very 60s geometric, linework star in teal blue and black and was an enormously popular design. My parents were gifted pieces of this design when they married in 1968 and it was still in use well into the 80s.
* 'Tempo' (also known as 'Carnaby') 1972–77: Swirling 60s psychedelic floral design in browns, teals, greens and oranges, this is the set that my paternal grandmother, Ada Bilson, served her famous Sunday roasts on. I have equal measure of nostalgia and fear when I see this design.
* 'Market Garden'/'Tuscany' 1971–82: Illustrations of vegetables such as beets, corn, tomatoes and cauliflowers. This is the set that we use at home.

SODASTREAM

Although commercial carbonation machines were invented in 1903 by Guy Hugh Gilbey and sold to the upper classes (including the Royal Family), a domestic version of the sodastream was not produced until 1955. They increased in popularity in the UK during the 70s and 80s when making carbonated (fizzy) drinks at home became attractive, with the 1979 advertising slogan 'Get busy with the fizzy'. There is a huge amount of nostalgia surrounding vintage sodastreams, and provided you can get an original canister there is very little that can go wrong with them. Even the glass bottles designed to be used in the machines are iconic and collectable with their swirling sides and white plastic screw tops.

Dorothy Jessie Tait

Dorothy, known as Jessie, was a creative ceramic designer who was born in Stoke-on-Trent and worked in the pottery industry. After studying at the Burslem School of Art, Tait first worked as a junior designer under Charlotte Rhead, and then went on to design for Midwinter between 1946 and 1974. Her designs during this period are considered to be the most well-known. She later moved to Johnson Brothers, part of the Wedgwood group who bought Midwinter in 1970. Tait retired in the early 90s.

HOW I CREATED

A RETRO KITCHEN

One thing I really struggled with was finding a vintage kitchen. We knew that we always wanted one to complete the look of the house, but try as we might, we couldn't find one the right size, or with the right number of cupboards, or in good enough condition to warrant ripping out a perfectly serviceable kitchen with one that was nearly 50 years old.

While bathrooms can easily be salvaged, the thing with kitchens is that they are used a lot every day but are made from chipboard and laminate, which do not usually fare well over the years. I still dream of a vintage orange and white kitchen, complete with track lighting (I have that waiting in the loft). I also dream of bold, bright, original tiles, but these are usually impossible to find new, and in the quantity that you need. You can salvage used tiles, but they too have their issues. That isn't to say that this isn't possible, but to assemble the component parts I feel that you need to be able to buy and store them ready for construction to commence in one fell swoop.

I mulled over this for some time – years, in fact. How could I achieve my retro kitchen without the drama, upheaval and expense of ripping out, what essentially is a great, well-made kitchen? My only option was paint; so

paint it was. This was in no way quick or easy, but it was most definitely worth the effort as we now have a kitchen, and although not vintage 70s, it looks retro enough for me to be satisfied until one day I stumble upon my perfect original one and a job lot of tiles that match.

We started by cleaning the cupboard units so that they were completely clean and grease free and used chalk paint to cover them and then a lacquer sealant to prevent the paint from damage. It also gave us the soft sheen look of an original kitchen. I opted for white and yellow, which were popular colours in 70s kitchens, and look fresh and inviting as well as clean and bright. We changed the handles to very simple chrome strips, ones which we felt were as close to something you would have had at the time. To complete the 70s look, we used one of our own designs of vinyl in a flooring quality on the worktops, and it's held up incredibly well with day to day use. The old adage 'Fake it till you make it' is definitely a phrase to use with regard to this kitchen. It's not original, but it looks a whole lot more in keeping with the overall style in our house.

BOLD CLASHING PATTERNS ON THE WALLPAPER AND CURTAINS WORK IN THIS BEDROOM AS THEY SHARE THE SAME COLOUR PALETTE, WHICH, MIXED WITH THE BAMBOO AND MACRAMÉ, GIVES A BOHEMIAN NOD TO THE STYLING WHICH WAS POPULAR IN THE DECADE. AN OLD LAMINATE SET OF DRAWERS HAS BEEN UPLIFTED WITH RETRO VINYL AND PROVIDES EXCELLENT STORAGE FOR CHILDREN'S BOOKS.

Drexel

If you are a fan of flower power, then you may like one of my favourite 70s bedroom sets, 'Drexel Plus One'. It is manufactured by the American company Drexel which designed the set after polling readers of *Seventeen* magazine to find out what they wanted from a bedroom set. Drexel worked with 3M, which made all of the fabulous vinyl that the pieces are covered in, depicting days of the week on clothes drawers, and even 'Bed' on the bedhead and 'Goodnight' on the bedside tables. The set is completed with daisy mirrors, butterfly tables and matching daisy details throughout, such as hand pulls. Although whimsical and not to everyone's taste, there is no denying which decade these pieces were produced in.

One of the many challenges of bedrooms is where to keep clothing. Wardrobes and chests of drawers are essential in the UK, where walk-in closets are rare. It's great that these items regularly appear for sale, and often as part of bedroom sets, complete with everything you need. Frequently these are listed cheaply on local selling pages as bulky items, such as wardrobes, are not easy for most vintage dealers to store.

Another thing that most people overlook these days when buying bedroom furniture but which instantly makes a bedroom look the part is the good old-fashioned dressing table: a brilliant bit of furniture which neatly stores everything from your underwear to make up and perfume/aftershave. There is something really extravagant about getting ready in front of a large purpose-built piece of furniture with a dedicated mirror and stool. Dressing tables come in all shapes and sizes, from compact ones like our own Stag piece, designed by Sylvia and John Reid, which will fit comfortably into a chimney nook, to large stately pieces by brands such as White & Newton or built-in storage solutions by companies such as Schreiber.

Bedrooms

Wood cladding was popular in the 60s and 70s and adds warmth to a room. Laura, @savagehouse1970, has styled her bedroom to simple boutique-hotel perfection with crisp white linen, teak bed and units, plants and stretched Marimekko fabric above the bed, proving that second-hand can be stylish – see page 147 for how to stretch your own vintage fabric.

HOW I CREATED

A 70S BEDROOM

Bedrooms are a place for sanctuary and restful sleep, but this doesn't mean that they should be calm and serene with pale, muted colours. You can decorate with a sense of energy and fun. I wanted to design my bedroom in a way that made me feel excited and energized for the day ahead as soon as I woke up. Traditionally, master bedrooms were decorated in a very feminine way with lots of frills and frou frou. However, from the 50s right through to the 70s, designs became starker and more streamlined with more graphic wallcoverings and brighter colours before being overtaken by the understated beige of the 80s. A flick through vintage design books from this era shows that bedrooms definitely become a place for 'adult fun', while children's rooms were full of whimsical ideas, painted murals and funky beds. It seems sad that this has mostly been lost to an excess of primarily grey and beige rooms which may be understated, but lack personality. The most important aspect of any bedroom must, of course, be the bed on which you will sleep: this will no doubt be the largest piece of furniture in the room and the layout will be dictated by it.

Our bed is a James Secombe space-age plastic modular bed, which is rumoured to have appeared on the set of a James Bond film. It definitely has that feeling to it with its smoked mirrored glass bedside tables which add an air of glamour and jet-set lifestyle. Because it is plastic, the bed was easy to clean, ready for us to use, but what about the crazy *Boogie Nights*-style upholstered

beds that sometimes come up for sale? Being fabric, these would have been tricky to clean but it is entirely possible to have these sanitized and deep steam-cleaned before using them. Alternatively, there are many independent upholsterers that would take on the challenge to recover them in a fabric of your choice. If going vintage with a bed isn't for you, then it is perfectly reasonable to use a modern divan; you could cover the base with fabric or even carpet and get a groovy headboard to create the look.

Although the bright pink swirling wallpaper and neon green in our own bedroom may be a bit much for some people, this bold palette has by far been my favourite incarnation on this room. If you want to create some interest and a focal point to a room, bold retro wallpaper on the bedhead wall will provide that instantly.

Everyone loves the idea of a clean and cosy bed to crawl into and layering of throws and cushions is another way to bring texture and colour into a room. Actress Faye Dunaway famously used a Greek flokati rug as a bedspread and, having tried this, it is indeed a fabulous and luxurious look. Soft furnishings in bedrooms can be tricky to get right – there's always the option to go full-on 70s with flowery sheets, clashing wallpaper and curtains. But to achieve a pared-back, modern look, reminiscent of a boutique hotel, I love a plain-coloured, high thread count, quality, 100% cotton bedding set. To me this screams luxury – and it feels like luxury, too, when you climb into bed after a long day.

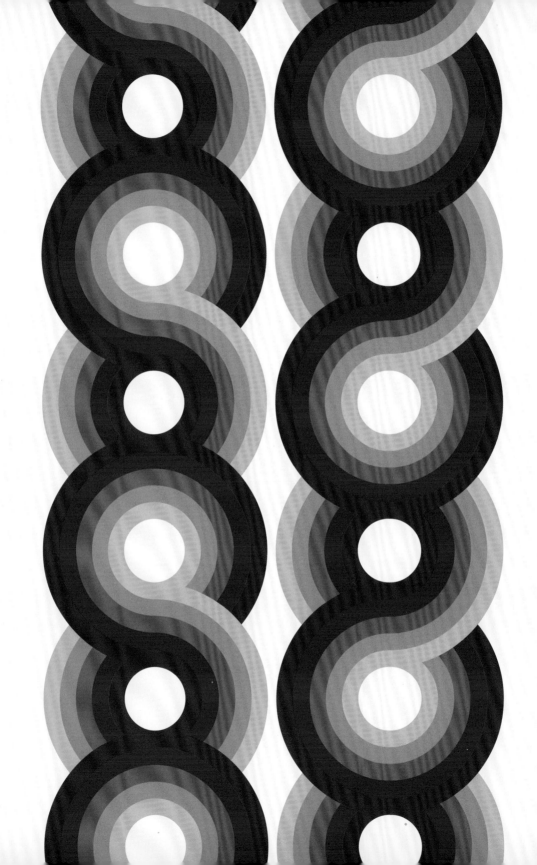

BRINGING THE 70s HOME

"Choosing colours should not be a gamble, it should be a conscious decision. Colours have a meaning and a function." VERNER PANTON

10 key looks

1. SIDEBOARD

A common feature of many homes, sideboards are traditionally placed in the dining room for displaying food and housing additional storage for cutlery and plates. Today they have a range of uses in various parts of the home, from hiding away ugly television boxes in the living room, to housing a record collection, children's toys, or even a mini bar for cocktail soirées. We have one on our landing to store bed linen! They are basically the perfect storage solution, effectively hiding all your clutter that you don't want to see, yet can't bear to throw away. The flat top of the sideboard is also incredibly useful for displaying treasured pieces – a lamp, a small collection of pottery or glass, or an attractive plant. A sideboard can bring a natural focal point to the room and really finish the look. They are easy to come across, buy the best you can afford and treasure it.

2. RECORD PLAYER AND VINYL

The 70s were the height of hi-fi and stereo equipment. The quality and sound mean that the hi-fi is still incredibly sought after by audiophiles today as superior to some modern equipment. Even mid-range hi-fis in the 70s were made incredibly well and sound great. There are many ways to purchase vintage set ups and specialists who will refurbish them too. Vinyl records can still be found freely for very little, although some artists and albums fetch large sums. The thrill of the chase is in finding beauties in piles of vinyl at car boot sales, in-between *Mrs Mills Piano Singalong* and copies of *Top of the Pops*. Shimmy over to page 168 to check out some of the best-selling albums of the decade.

3. SHAG PILE

Nothing sums up the decade more than a shaggy rug or carpet. They instantly create that 70s vibe when walking into a room, and the brighter the better. Even though original ones are getting harder to find and more expensive, you can still find them. Greek flokati rugs are still made and sold today and are real investment pieces. Check out page 139 for the history behind these rugs and what to look for when buying a vintage piece.

4. WEST GERMAN POTTERY

Iconic to the decade was a type of pottery from West Germany with typically bright colours and patterns and a 'lava' glaze that gives pieces a distinctive bubbling effect. Go for a striking light with a conical shade or display a collection of vases in odd numbers in varying shapes and sizes for a polished look. Pop your house plants in an attractive lava pot to accentuate its beauty. You can still pick up basic designs from thrift stores or car boot sales for very little money. Take a look at page 57 for more details on West German pottery.

5. BOLD WALLCOVERINGS

If you want that 70s look for your home and to create an instant statement do not shy away when it comes to painting or decorating your room. Anything goes but the bigger, bolder and brighter, the better. If you can't face the whole room being in a bright colour, then you can tone it down with warm white or magnolia walls. Our wallpaper, sold on www.70shousemanchester.com, allows you to get the look instantly without trying to track down multiple rolls of vintage wallpaper. Supergraphic wall murals are an easy and cost-effective way to bring retro design into your home (see page 50). There are lots of hints and tips on how to use colour and pattern in your home on pages 108-11.

6. PENDANT LIGHTING

Lighting was big in the 70s with all sorts of crazy designs. Large, diffused glass shades in bold colours, or white milk glass, dangling in multiples over a dining table, in the centre of a living room or over a stairwell can create an impact and scream that retro look. Lights that can retract up or extend down are a useful addition when eating to create that authentic mood. Look on auction sites for original examples which are sometimes far cheaper than modern equivalents. Check out page 130 for more information.

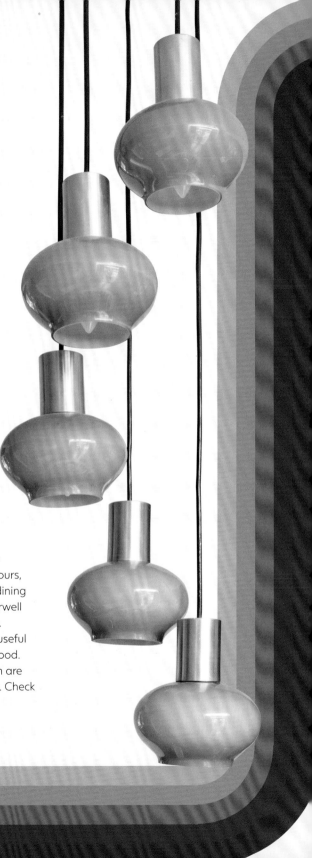

7. CHEESE PLANT

If there is one plant that sums up the decade it would have to be the Swiss cheese plant, or to give it its scientific name, *Monstera deliciosa*. Its attractive cut away leaves and ability to grow to huge proportions can really add interest to a room. One of these will make a statement and always will be talked about.

Swiss cheese plants are now fairly easy to track down at your local supermarket, garden centre or IKEA. Look at page 47 to see more about caring for these and other 70s beauties.

8. TULIP CHAIR

The original 'Tulip' chair, as it is known, was designed by Eero Saarinen for Knoll in 1956. It was originally part of the 'Pedestal' collection, and it revolutionized modernist furniture design.

Such was the popularity of the space-age swivel design that it continued to be used throughout the next two decades with other versions bring produced, including variations by Lusch Erzeugnis for Hille International in the 60s and Maurice Burke for Arkana in the 70s. Their sleek and timeless design works well in retro and modern interiors. Find out more about space-age designs on pages 66-9.

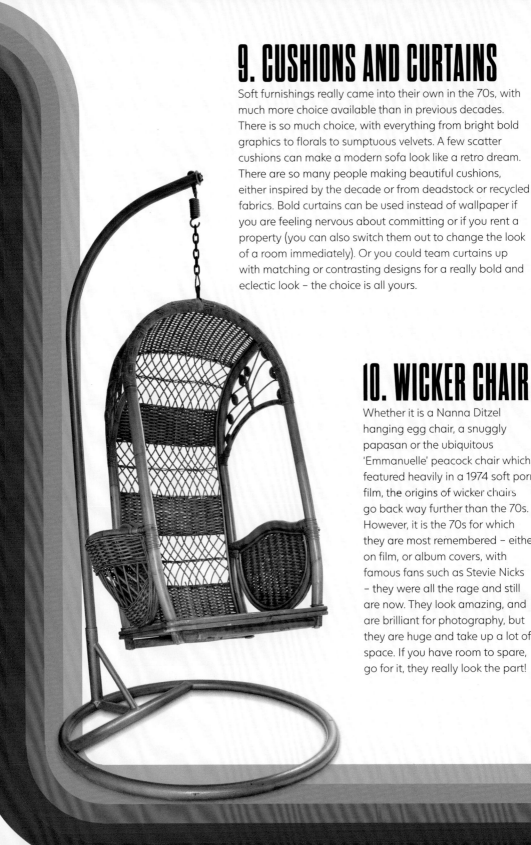

9. CUSHIONS AND CURTAINS

Soft furnishings really came into their own in the 70s, with much more choice available than in previous decades. There is so much choice, with everything from bright bold graphics to florals to sumptuous velvets. A few scatter cushions can make a modern sofa look like a retro dream. There are so many people making beautiful cushions, either inspired by the decade or from deadstock or recycled fabrics. Bold curtains can be used instead of wallpaper if you are feeling nervous about committing or if you rent a property (you can also switch them out to change the look of a room immediately). Or you could team curtains up with matching or contrasting designs for a really bold and eclectic look – the choice is all yours.

10. WICKER CHAIR

Whether it is a Nanna Ditzel hanging egg chair, a snuggly papasan or the ubiquitous 'Emmanuelle' peacock chair which featured heavily in a 1974 soft porn film, the origins of wicker chairs go back way further than the 70s. However, it is the 70s for which they are most remembered – either on film, or album covers, with famous fans such as Stevie Nicks – they were all the rage and still are now. They look amazing, and are brilliant for photography, but they are huge and take up a lot of space. If you have room to spare, go for it, they really look the part!

Colour, pattern, and style

A comfy, oversized 'Pacer' chair in burnt orange in the home of Sarah @retro-saz.

Our home has evolved over a long period of time. Did I get it right first time? No. Is it perfect now? Still no. There are always elements that I would tweak or change.

Decorating and styling your home using vintage furniture and accessories takes time and perseverance, but finding your treasured pieces will make you appreciate the love, patience and dedication you have put into your home. Finding pieces you love, that make your heart sing, and the story behind where you found them will be entwined in the very fabric of your interiors. Whatever style you choose, whether you purchase items from a vintage dealer, a thrift store or inherit them from a family member, you will be safe in the knowledge that no one else has quite the same style as you do. As I said at the start, the photographs and suggestions are to inspire and not to dictate. There are no rules about how to style and decorate your own space; many interior designers will use rules to create balance which I will elaborate on, but the most important part of any design within your home is to make it joyful and a place where you want to spend time with friends and family.

Top tip
When shopping for vintage take a tape measure and make a note of the size of the space you have available to you, also think about how you will get it in your home. Our hall is very narrow with a turn, this makes it pretty much impossible to get bigger items in the house through this entrance so we use the back doors. I learnt this lesson multiple times the hard way with beds stuck at strange angles in the door of my flat, the purchase of a jukebox some 15 years ago which resulted in taking the front door off its hinges at 8pm, I never seem to learn though when I see something fabulous...

WHERE TO START?

No doubt if you are new to decorating and interior design the whole process can feel overwhelming, and I can understand this. Sometimes I feel the same when I want to decorate a room, but some of the best advice I can give is to paint it white and LIVE in the space. Take notice of what time of day the sun hits the room; is it the cool early morning light or the warm evening sunsets? Where are the light and shadows? Are there any elements of the room that make it an awkward shape which could be easily rectified? Think about your needs for the room – do you need storage for clothing, toys, cookware? What furniture do you need or desire in the room, a dining table, sofa, sideboard? Once you have a rough idea of your requirements and sizes you can start to plan a list of items you would like to look for and the budget you have available.

HOW TO PLAN A ROOM

Unless you are a professional interior designer, or can afford to hire one, then chances are that you are going to be planning your room yourself or with a partner in crime. My partner in crime when planning a room isn't necessarily my long-suffering partner in life, mostly because I tend to change and adapt my ideas over the planning stage and he starts to object to fanciful ideas that I want, but maybe can't have or afford. A room goes through various levels of editing before I start to decorate, so I find a trusted friend who shares my aesthetic is a good sounding board for wild flights of fancy. Having said that, if you are very fixed on an idea and know in your heart that it is perfect then don't be swayed by someone else and GO FOR IT!

BE INSPIRED

How I plan to decorate a room probably isn't correct in the terms of professionals, but it's always worked for me. I am a deep thinker with a huge imagination, and I love times where I can just sit and let ideas pop into my head, or consider how I can adapt an idea I've been inspired by and make it work within our space and budget.

Inspiration comes from many places – seeing other people's homes in books and magazines, or online with resources such as Pinterest, where you can search and save ideas easily for future reference. It is worth keeping the ideas you love in one place where you can refer back to them; you might be years away from designing a garden, but if you love something you've seen it's nice to be able to find it again. For me, I really enjoy looking back at old magazines and books. I love nothing more than sourcing a DIY or interiors book from the 70s and flicking through the images to give me inspiration and place my own twist on it. I have compiled a resource list of books which are now out of print but can be found online from second-hand booksellers. I rarely purchase new magazines, preferring to buy vintage ones which have more of a stylistic interest to me.

WHAT'S YOUR MOOD?

I know that a lot of designers, both professional and amateur, make a huge deal out of mood boards, and yes, they are absolutely needed for an interior designer to present to a client. Are they needed for you to decorate your own home? Not really. Pictures placed on paper or on a screen may help some people visualize colours and ideas, but I know a lot of people who are fearful of mood boards and feel that they aren't doing it right and worry that this is a necessary part of the process and that they have failed at the first hurdle. Sticking pictures you have cut out of a magazine isn't a mood board, despite what some people will tell you.

Instead think BIG – get large swatches where you can, pin them to your walls, lay them out on your floors, touch them, see them, live with them, stroke them, sniff them! Immerse yourself in the colours and textures and note how these make you feel. Decorating your home should make you feel like you're in love; it should make you feel excited; it shouldn't feel like a chore.

COLOUR

For the early part of the decade on-trend colours were bright greens, pops of turquoise, sunshine yellows, punchy pinks, regal purples and of course the colours that everyone associates with the era: orange and brown.

Often people will tell me they love our interiors, and would want something similar themselves, but are scared to try the bright, bold colours. My advice here would be to start small. Begin by introducing colour via accessories such as rugs, curtains etc, this way you can learn to live with bold accents. This is especially useful if you are living in rented accommodation which cannot be redecorated. Once you feel comfortable living with some colour, it is easier to branch out of your comfort zone, taking things at your own pace and budget. It is fine to make mistakes (almost no one gets things right first time) and if you hate something, it's not the end of the world. It is better to regret the things you did than live in fear of the things you wanted to try.

The 60-30-10 rule

... is a timeless, failsafe guide to balancing colours, using percentages.

60 per cent is the predominant room colour, usually a neutral.
30 per cent is a secondary supporting colour, perhaps a bold accent wall, curtains or furniture.
10 per cent is an accent colour, using accessories, cushions, artworks etc.

There are so many shades that it can get very confusing – a colour that looks amazing in the store might look overwhelming, or flat or dull in your home. When testing out hues for a room, bring home colour chips from the shop, tape these to walls and select ones you are drawn to the most. Then get some cheap lining paper and paint huge sections in the colours you are drawn to, using tester pots. This allows you to see large areas of the paint, how the light affects the colour and how it works with your existing furniture and accessories. It also lets you move the colour swatch around the room with ease to check different walls. (This is also a great idea if you don't wish to live with random paint patches all over your room until it is time to decorate.) You can live with the colour for a while and see how this affects you: does it excite you, make you calm, or happy? I also advocate the same technique for wallpaper, trying the largest sample you can, if unsure.

Top Tip
Find a fabulous piece of vintage fabric or wallpaper you love and use this as inspiration for your colour scheme: the fabric designer has already done the hard work for you, selecting colours that work together. You can even get the paint colours matched at your local hardware store.

DEVELOP YOUR STYLE

Your own style is something unique to you and will naturally change over the course of the years. I know myself that things I loved ten years ago don't necessarily excite me as much now, and this is the beauty of vintage items which can be sold on when your time with them is done. As you decorate and become more confident in your knowledge, choice of items and overall style, this will evolve naturally. The urge to collect and display everything will mellow into editing your collections into the pieces you love most. Some you will love and treasure and will always be a mainstay of your interior design; others will change. Some items I envisage treasuring forever are large investment pieces such as my Axminster rug (see page 140); in the same length of time we have owned the rug we have had four sideboards and as many sofas, all vintage, which were sold to create space for something that worked better for us.

Popular colour combinations of the time included tones of:

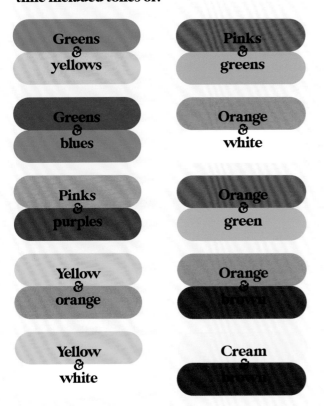

Greens & yellows

Greens & blues

Pinks & purples

Yellow & orange

Yellow & white

Pinks & greens

Orange & white

Orange & green

Orange & brown

Cream & brown

What are 70s colours?

The 70s was a unique and bold time for decorating at home, a period where people born post war were settling with families and decorating homes for the first time and there were some interesting choices! The pale and more subtle colours of the 50s and early 60s gave way to louder and brighter colours of the late 60s with their psychedelic hues, progressing through the 70s to softer, more natural colours.

* White, as a neutral, was used everywhere from walls to floors to furniture to offset the bright colours; similarly black was used as an accent. Cream colours were also incredibly popular, along with the much-maligned magnolia, which, used in context, is a wonderfully warm neutral, poles apart from its reputation of epitomizing homes lacking in style, new builds and uninspired rentals.

* Bringing the outside in was a popular choice with the textural use of bricks, stone, wood panelling and cork (which subsequent home owners ripped out in the ensuing decades).

* Tonality was huge, with most opting to paint their homes in shades of the

My thoughts on woodchip wallpaper

It might have been popular in the 70s, but quite frankly it's the devil's work. It is the antithesis of anything stylish and a pain to remove from walls. If there is one thing that should be relegated to the decade never to return, it should be this.

same colour, applied to walls, ceilings and woodwork; people wanted the maximum amount of colour and patterns possible within each room.

✱ Supergraphics (see page 50) were used around the home, offering a modern twist to traditional wallpaper for some. Bold wallpaper was still a very popular choice for many, and not restricted to one wall, but covering entire rooms. Foil wallpapers and murals of nature scenes such as beaches or mountains were also popular, yet avant-garde choices, creating focal points and talking points within a room.

✱ As the 70s progressed, the colours became more earthy. By the middle of the decade rich shades including the legendary 'avocado', 'linden' and warmer more muted orange shades such as 'cinnamon' were paired with 'bamboo' and were listed on colour cards along with exotic names such as 'lime juice', 'poppy' and 'sultan'. By the end of the decade and towards the 80s, subtle changes in style moved towards the Italian, subdued shades of creams, browns and whites, which were used in conjunction with hints of colour in predominately pale rooms.

WHERE TO FIND VINTAGE WALLPAPERS

You can still buy vintage wallpaper if you have a look online; often you are limited by the number of rolls available, sometimes single or even part rolls, meaning only small space can be decorated. Where large quantities of exceptional designs are found, the prices reflect this.

Owing to the nature of paper, it can degrade over time which means that vintage wallpaper sometimes cannot be hung correctly, or it disintegrates or is stained along the edges. I have experienced all of these issues hanging vintage wallpaper over the years.

The good news is that some large established companies are looking back in their archives and reissuing retro designs and other small businesses are working hard to develop their own take on retro design. We started looking into producing small-batch wallpaper in early 2020 when people online kept asking where we got our wallpaper from. We are slowly building up a portfolio of designs where we work with UK-based designers, factories and family businesses to make exciting designs inspired by the 70s available for you to have in your own homes.

Back in the 70s, gardens were serious business. Recalling my own grandfather's garden, you wouldn't see an unkempt lawn or flowers that needed dead-heading; it was very much a keeping up with the Joneses affair.

The inside of homes may have been full of shag pile and orange, but the outside was still very much the preserve of the post-war aesthetic, with everything very regimented. Everything had its place, from the from formal parks and flower beds, to the veggie plot in the back corner, with roses, dahlias and sweet peas blooming alongside roses and lavender. Sheds were very much for tools and the occasional deck chair, or orange and brown daisy-patterned sun lounger that had a tendency either to trap your fingers or collapse when you were lying on it. Outdoor spaces had yet to catch on as an extension of the indoor, as we see them now, and so more eclectic styles were not curated.

CREATE A RETRO-STYLE GARDEN

* **Breeze blocks** – DIY or builders' suppliers still stock the traditional La Costa (flower shape) block but you can find lots of reclaimed ones including La Costa, La Fiesta and square on square at low cost on places like Facebook Marketplace, as people have a tendency to get rid of these when modernizing their gardens. You can even ask neighbours directly to save them for you if you know they are having building work done.

* **Colour** – Bring the inside outside with the use of bright tropical hues for that retro Palm Springs/Miami/Butlin's vibe.

* **Accessories** – From kitsch gnomes, to plastic flamingos and reclaimed concrete planters, all add to that kitsch retro aesthetic.

* **Seating** – We have used modern replicas of the iconic S-shaped 'Panton' chair; the plastic means that they can be kept outside without fear of damage.

* **Patio** – A paved area used for dining was included in many 70s houses and when styled can look very retro.

* **Swinging chair with canopy** – Sadly our garden is too small to house one of these, but I have always lusted over them!

* **Vintage chairs and parasols** – One of the easiest ways to give the 70s feel to a garden instantly is with original garden accessories in bright and bold floral prints – you can find these easily on auction sites.

* **Lighting** – Ditch the tasteful warm white festoons and go multi-coloured to give it that 70s Spanish taberna feel.

* **Plants** – Retro plants like fuchsias, sweet peas, roses, dahlias and petunias, aren't just pretty, they help the bees too.

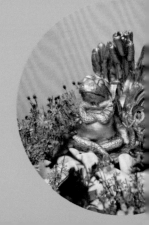

Furniture

PARKER KNOLL & SWIVEL CHAIRS

Parker Knoll has its roots back in Victorian England, set up in 1869 by Fredrick Parker whose desire to create the finest furnishings available, even led to the company furnishing ocean liners such as the RMS *Aquitania* and RMS *Queen Mary* during the early part of the twentieth century.

Parker Knoll are perhaps most well known for their 1969 classic 'Statesman'. Originally designed as contract furniture for the office and board room, it made the leap from office to home office to lounge in the 70s. With new technologies in reclining chairs in the 60s, this sexy beast of a chair both tilted and swivelled from its chrome pedestal base. Available in many fabrics from the business-like black leather to softer draylon (a type of fabric with velvet-like properties) in a range of colours and with additional pieces such as a matching footstool and three-seater sofa, this was the ultimate 'man-about-the-house' aspirational seating of the 70s.

This contemporary design which wowed at furniture exhibitions in the 70s is still as fresh and relevant in the twenty-first century, with a version of it still made by Parker Knoll today.

Original chairs from the 70s are still very much in demand, as are similar chairs made by Vono, Greaves & Thomas and G Plan with their model 6250 chair, also known as the 'Blofeld' chair after the James Bond villain who used it in the 1967 film *You Only Live Twice*. Inspired by Arne Jacobsen's earlier 'Egg' chair, it was marketed as 'The world's most comfortable chair', and it certainly lives up to its slogan. Many of these chairs retain their original upholstery, but don't be put off by a shabbier example at a lower price as there are many modern upholsterers who specialize in refurbishing vintage chairs so that they will have another 50 years of life.

NATHAN

This British brand had the reputation of being up-market and traditional, with an emphasis on quality and craftmanship. Nathan was a follower of trends rather than a leader, catering largely for the more mature homeowner.

The brand's first range, 'Citadel' was advertised in the mid-60s. By the early 70s, the market was saturated with teak furniture, distinctive design choices were made to stand out from the crowd including geometric marquetry veneered doors on a stripped-back simple design, complete with its own drinks cabinet for the ubiquitous cocktail party. This was called 'Circles', designed by Patrick Lee for Nathan, and is now incredibly sought after with prices for restored versions often reaching over £1,000 ($1,200). Other designs are the 'Trinity' coffee table, with three individual side tables and stools that slot neatly under a glass top, and their teak bentwood/thermoformed and glass tables, which included a drop-down central 'bar' feature. The latter pushed the boundaries of contemporary design and still looks refreshingly modern today. Most common is their teak and glass coffee table which resembles a Reuleaux triangle. I own one of these, which I found in 2002 in a local refuge centre for a few pounds. Such is the price rise and interest in furniture of the era that these pieces often now fetch over £150 ($200). Similar to the success that G Plan had with 'Fresco' in the late 60s and early 70s, Nathan found favour with their traditionally styled 'Jacobean' range – a fussier and more detailed frontage for a new era. It is noted that by 1975 the retail prices of Nathan were far cheaper than their main competitors and the quality was certainly lacking in places. Nathan Furniture is still readily available today from second-hand markets for varying prices. It is not quite as desirable in some cases as G Plan, especially the 70s 'Jacobean' design which seems to dominate by sheer volume.

ROOM DIVIDERS

Room dividers help to zone spaces in open-plan living and double up as great storage if they have units below.

Brands such as Stonehill and Schreiber offer stylish options at budget prices. Although not strictly 70s, pieces such as the Ercol 'Giraffe', will set you back well over £1,000 ($1,300). Dividers can be purely decorative too, more like screens, with examples by Czech designer Ludvik Volak often reaching £2,000 ($2,500) in today's market. My own divider is a hefty modernist bentwood version that I purchased on series 2 of *The Bidding Room*, and although it isn't exactly a useful piece of furniture in the sense of storage it adds interest and depth to the space. The researchers for the show and I have yet to attribute the design to anyone. I certainly have never seen one previously, and it may be a one-off. One day I might find out, but until then, I will bask in its beautiful, yet fairly useless charm.

LADDERAX

I am often asked about our modular shelving unit in the dining room which houses various collections and our vinyl records. This is an example of the popular Ladderax shelving system, originally created in Cricklewood, London, in 1964 and comprising metal or wood 'ladders', hooked metal fixings and shelves or units.

The concept was inspired by Scandinavian designs such as the String shelving system developed by Nisse and Kajsa Strinning. The main advantage of Ladderax over its European counterparts is that it is incredibly flexible in its unique ladder construction which consist of two options: a free-standing version, and one that has feet at the front and the back and counterbalances against the wall; this completely negates the need to permanently attach wooden brackets to the walls, making them flexible enough to add, subtract or move around as required. The bonus of this is that it is relatively easy to start collecting a Ladderax system by simply starting with two uprights, some metal rods and shelves. Once

you have this basic set up you can begin to increase your ladders and units when finances allow. There are two heights of ladder, with cabinet options including glass-fronted cabinets, drawer units, record cabinets, bureaus and cocktail bars.

Ladderax was incredibly popular, so vintage pieces are readily available to purchase; a quick search online will bring up a large selection of options. If you do find a bargain deal, don't delay, others are on the look out for these very desirable storage solutions. Prices have increased considerably over the past five years; once you could purchase three bays with rods and units for around £300 ($350), this has since rocketed to over £1,000 ($1,300). That isn't to say that bargains can't still be found; I came across a darker-stained, single bay version a couple of years ago for only £20 ($25) as it was listed simply as 'shelves'.

If wall storage is your bag but you can't afford the price tag there are other options available. Often huge wall units from brands such as G Plan or Nathan, or similar appear online very inexpensively.

PIEFF

Started by Fred and David Bates as a contract furniture manufacturer in 1953 called Production Facilities Ltd, the company initially supplied mostly canteen furniture. It wasn't until David's younger brother, Tim, joined the company in the mid-60s that they started working towards changing their designs for a high-end audience. Tim Bates' first collection debuted in May 1970, coinciding with the change of company name to Pieff, which became one of the leading furniture manufacturers during the 70s.

Often used in luxury hotels, embassies and even royal palaces, Pieff pieces used the highest quality materials and workmanship. Nearly 50 years later their 70s pieces still look remarkably modern today.

Sold only in exclusive furniture shops such as Heal's and Harrods, Pieff's unique style was characterized by smooth chrome, very much in the style of Swiss-French architect Le Corbusier, with leather or cut velvet upholstery. They used deep smoked glass on their tables, Brazilian rosewood (which has been protected as an endangered species since 1992) and Pirelli webbing on their sofas.

By the height of their popularity in the mid-70s, you could spot Pieff's luxurious designs on hit television series such as *This Is Your Life*; the popular British science-fiction soap opera *Blake's 7*; and – one of my personal favourites – *The Good Life*, in the dining room of Margo and Jerry Leadbetter.

Today Pieff pieces look just as good styled with vintage or contemporary pieces and are a perfect example of post-modern style of the decade. Designs to look for include 'Eleganza', chrome cantilever-style dining chairs with high backs, and the sister design 'Lisse'. Coffee tables including the rare 'Edel' design with coiled spring legs and their range of 'Alpha', 'Beta' and 'Gamma' sofas, all polished tubular chrome with a low slung and laid-back look. The 'Mandarin' sofas with their more angular square chrome frame and over-stuffed upholstery is the height of mid-70s style.

Top Tip

When purchasing Ladderax, check out the individual parts, some of these are purely cosmetic and can be remedied easily, such as rusted shelving rods or splashes of paint which can be easily cleaned. More expensive damage that is harder to fix would be damaged veneer, missing parts, locked units with missing keys, which should be reflected in the price.

Top Tip

Check the rubber Pirelli webbing on the Pieff sofa seats, as these can sometimes perish with age and break and it is difficult to find replacements.

MARCEL BREUER'S LONG CHAIR

One piece of furniture that I had to include in my first book would be one of my most treasured possessions: a long chair, designed by Marcel Breuer.

Breuer (1902–81) was a Hungarian-born designer, a protégé of Bauhaus founder Walter Gropius and champion of the modern movement. Celebrated both in furniture and architecture, he revolutionized modern interiors with his iconic tubular steel furniture collection, inspired by bicycle construction. His designs remain some of the most identifiable pieces of the twentieth century. Bauhaus style and Marcel Breuer designs had a massive resurgence in the late 60s and throughout the 70s thanks partly to the revival of Isokon Furniture, but also to Knoll (distinct from Parker Knoll) for purchasing his entire catalogue and re-releasing designs, including the famous 'Wassily' long chair. Habitat also started selling reproductions of the 'Cesca' chair. You can see a photo, including the long chair, in the home of David Hockney in Terence Conran's *The House Book*.

Breuer emigrated to the UK, and worked for a short time with Isokon, developing his long chair in 1935. A bentwood frame of laminated birch supporting a shaped timber seat and back, its moulded plywood design is one of the earliest examples, along with ones by Finnish architect Alvar Aalto, of 'organic' furniture. Breuer's design of the long chair spreads a person's weight across a larger surface area, giving greater comfort and support. Isokon advertised it for their launch in 1936 as 'giving scientific relaxation for every part of the body, immediately creating a feeling of well-being'.

London based Isokon was founded in 1929, but ceased production by 1939. Having never been a commercial success and hampered by the Second World War, the company was restarted again, in 1963, producing in the UK, and since 1982 furniture has been made by Isokon Plus. During the 60s my father worked in London as a cabinet maker and production manager, and worked closely with the manufacturers who were licensed to produce Isokon pieces. He managed not only to acquire a long chair, but also several other pieces, including a small coffee table and Penguin Donkey Mk2 designed by Ernest Race. Throughout my childhood the long chair was present; there are photos of me standing beside it. I have memories of my father lying on it and listening to records on his headphones. I remember him listening to 'Imagine' by John Lennon with tears in his eyes, trying to explain to me that someone had just shot that man.

Through unforeseen circumstances my family had to sell the chair, which I knew my father always regretted. Even as a child I said that when I was a grown up, I would buy another one. Over the years I looked but they were always out of my price range, until one day in 2018 I looked online and there was one, five miles from me, with a very low starting bid, stupidly low... It wasn't in the best condition, but I could afford it (just). My heart pounded as I placed the opening bid, which was my highest limit, and no one else had bid, so it was mine. I immediately called my dad and told him what I had bought and he offered to restore the frame for me and I reupholstered it with loving care.

MERROW ASSOCIATES

Along with Pieff, this was another luxury British design-led company of the 70s. Launched in the 60s, it was the brainchild of Royal Academy graduate Richard Young. Like Pieff, the company made furniture using chromed steel, smoked glass and rosewood with their own distinctive style. It sold through a few very exclusive stores, including Harrods, and in Europe.

The range included dining and coffee tables, chairs, desks and sideboards. Pieces are highly sought after because few were made owing to the quality of design and make. Richard's son James relaunched the company in 2020.

I have had not one but two of their 341G 'Talbot' coffee tables in my time, both I bought stupidly cheap and sold on after a while; sadly one of my regrets in buying and selling.

Fact
Ronnie Corbett's famous chair on *The Two Ronnies* was designed and made by Merrow Associates.

SOFAS

One of the trickiest elements, and one which is key to any comfortable living area, is the humble sofa.

They are one of the hardest-working pieces of furniture in the home and, after 50 years of bums on seats, older sofas in original condition tend to suffer from issues such as sagging webbing, structural problems, dirty or discoloured upholstery, rips and general wear and tear. Vintage sofas generally fall into three categories:

1. Absolutely trashed, looks like a dog has eaten it.
2. Mint-condition designer piece which has never been touched.
3. Refurbished by a dealer.

It is possible to find some examples that remain immaculate through careful owners with rooms that were kept 'for best', so these are always worth looking at. There are complicated laws on second-hand upholstered items due to fire regulations, so it is tricky to source sofas which have all the fire regulation paperwork complete. As a result, many that have been donated end up in landfill as they cannot be resold by charities etc. Some specialist dealers will offer vintage pieces from the 70s for sale with original coverings, or ones which have been refurbished by themselves which will raise the retail cost. If you are looking for an original, then check out online auctions or local selling pages as you will likely find items within budget. If possible, check the item in person before bidding to ensure that it is structurally sound and comfortable. If you find a desirable piece, as I did with my old Skipper Møbler sofa, it is worth checking if the bones of the sofa are good enough to work with. Working with an upholsterer means that you will know that all of the sofa will meet with the stringent fire regulations.

We went through about three vintage sofas from the Skipper Møbler (lovely but too delicate for a small child to throw themselves around on); to a Pieff 'Alpha' – great to look at but not good to lie on due to the chrome base; to our final incarnation, an original 1975 G Plan sofa in bright green. To be honest, I wasn't looking to buy a sofa in this shade, but a dealer wanted to buy my Pieff so I sold it and panic bought this one via Facebook for £100 ($120). Turns out it was the best deal ever, not only is it in great condition but it is super comfortable too. G Plan sofas seem to last the test of time and appear on the market fairly often.

If buying a vintage sofa isn't something you want to commit to then there are lots of vintage-inspired designs on the market, with brands like G Plan offering heritage ranges from their archives in modern fabrics.

Lighting your home

Regardless of how you chose to furnish or style your home, the principles of lighting remain the same. Whether you're after task, ambient, directional, decorative or atmospheric lighting, the size and, to a degree, the shape of an area can be affected by lighting techniques, which can make or break a design scheme.

First and foremost, almost all domestic homes will come equipped with at least one pendant light flex, usually in the centre of the room, also known colloquially as THE BIG LIGHT. This single flex with a shade and with a 40-watt bulb is singularly the most depressing lighting known to mankind. It neither flatters yourself nor the room, nor illuminates. If you are starting a room from scratch, planning the lighting at the outset allows for greater flexibility later on, ensuring that you have the correct number of wall switches, chased-in cables (if you want wall sconces) and even whole lighting systems, which can be accessed from an app. Every room will need careful consideration with regard to usage, even multiple usage and power requirements. When choosing lighting, the first thing to ask yourself is whether it harmonizes with the general scheme. Will it be fit for purpose in the area you wish to use it and withstand normal domestic use (and abuse) from pets and children?

The 70s, for me, offered a huge wealth of choice, not only in accessible lighting, which is still readily available, but also in terms of design. High-end pieces of the time were watered down and copied for mass consumption through high-street stores. A quick browse online will yield many options to suit any budget, from a simple paper globe to beautiful Italian designer pieces – as with anything, buy what you love as you will be living with it.

Questions to think about

✳ How are you using the room?
✳ What type of light is needed? Direct, indirect, adjustable, strong or background?
✳ Will the light cast onto surfaces be adequate for your needs?
✳ Are there enough switches and power outlets, and are these in the correct position?
✳ If rewiring, have you worked out the best position for all the elements you need?
✳ What type of light fitting will suit the room?

Top Tip

Always purchase PAT-tested electrical items where possible, this means that they have been tested to be safe. Always use a qualified electrician to install lighting; there are many specialists who will rewire old lamps.

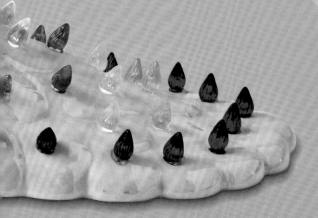

So, what to look for? Personally, I am a massive fan of staggered globe chandeliers; these hang in our living and dining areas at home and create a beautiful statement, lit or unlit. In the living room ours is placed on a dimmer switch for ambiance. We also have a selection of alternative lighting to use when we don't wish to switch on the mighty 'big light'. Our wall art behind the sofa doubles up as a light, casting dramatic shadows and a warm diffused glow from the back of the room. This gives the whole area a completely different feel, especially if we are entertaining and want more of a cocktail lounge vibe. We also have diffused pendant lights in the corner and small decorative globe pieces on our shelving, each highlighting different aspects of the room for different needs and uses. Our dining room has another staggered 70s chandelier, positioned centrally over our dining table, which gives a beautiful glow to the food that we are enjoying. These globes contain a white milk glass inner so the light is brighter than that given from a plain coloured glass shade. Additional pendant lighting gives task light to the record player; this also doubles up as mood lighting in the evenings if the main light is switched off, creating dramatic shadows from the plants placed in the space.

Uplighters are a useful addition in homes, enabling swathes of light to be projected up onto a specific area. These work beautifully placed behind a statement plant, such as 70s favourite the Swiss Cheese, to create a dramatic atmosphere. Lamps are so versatile; they can be moved and shades can be changed to suit interiors with ease. I love the huge, oversized floor lamps with tall 'witches' hat shades that are most commonly associated with the West German pottery factories, but imitated elsewhere. Over the years I have had many of these 'lava' design lamps, from huge squat pots that sit on the floor, to table-sized lamps – I cannot resist their Marmite nature. Love or loathe them they are truly statement lamps of the decade. Lamps are easy to come across, and vary in price from £10 ($13) upwards, depending on the condition, size and colour. The shade play an important part in the overall desirability and price, often being as much as the lamp base itself. If you happen across a reasonably priced lamp without a shade, fear not! There are many online retailers making them in various shapes, sizes and colours or using reclaimed vintage fabric.

LEFT, MY WEST GERMAN POTTERY LAMP HAS BRIGHT COLOURED GLAZES MIXED WITH DRIPPING 'LAVA' DESIGNS, DISTINCTIVE SIDE HANDLES AND SHAPED CUT-OUTS WITHIN THE BASE FOR AN ADDITIONAL LIGHT SOURCE.

Top Tip
Shades can provide a useful starting point for a whole room scheme from the colours and patterns used.

SPOTLIGHTS

Spotlights, particularly on portable poles, are a brilliant way of accessing task lighting and also creating directional lighting. They can also be decorative pieces of furniture in their own right, such as Terence Conran's Maclamps, which are suitable for desks, and 70s chromed versions which can be positioned on a central pole and are incredibly useful additions to the home. Eyeball spotlights, named after their spherical nature, are also beautiful yet useful modern collectables.

NOVELTY LIGHTING

That fine line where kitsch meets hideous, I am all for it. Light-up waterfall? Yes please. Fibre-optic flowers? Go on then… My collection includes a television lamp: a glorious technicolour peacock (see page 130), made simply and inexpensively out of a moulded ceramic base. They are similar in principle to ceramic Christmas trees that you can find and were often hand-crafted at ceramic decorating classes. I have rarely seen these in the UK, and they are most often found in the US, where mine is from. I often wonder how this ended up in a box, in a field at a car boot sale in Lancashire, purchased for only a few pounds. The seller probably thought I was mad, and maybe I am, but if your heart can't sing from a multcoloured light-up peacock then you're probably dead inside.

CANDLELIGHT

Don't underestimate the use of candlelight when setting the ambience of an interior, especially when entertaining or at festive times of the year. There are vast quantities of vintage candlesticks to suit every budge, from glass votives through to modular metal ones; group them together for dramatic effect.

NEON

Although neon lights go back to the turn of the twentieth century in commercial use, many associate their usage in the golden era of Las Vegas from the 50s to the 70s, and indeed the Neon Museum is a must if you ever visit the city. For the past few years, neon has been gaining in popularity in our homes via influencers. Modern neon lights are often mis-sold and are actually LED lighting, which is incredibly bad for the environment, as it is single-use plastic. My advice if you want to entertain neon in your home is to seek out a neon glass blower who will talk you through making a truly bespoke piece for your home; there are even courses on how to make your own neon gas light, which makes a great gift.

MUSHROOM LAMPS

Glass versions are attributed to Murano, with their distinctive wavy lines. These are harder to come across in second-hand shops, but can be found online. Plastic examples of Italian-produced Guzzini lights or period replicas can be found easily enough, although the prices are rising considerably. These acrylic globes were popular during the mid- to late 70s. Arc lamp versions of these are incredibly desirable and immediately take you back to the era. Possibly one of the most famous examples was designed in 1971, a collaboration between designers Verner Panton and Louis Poulsen to create the trumpet-based 'Panthella' light. Vintage pieces in chrome or off-white are highly collectable and are priced accordingly but you can buy a modern example of this design classic from places like The Conran Shop.

TENSION POLES

These are lamps attached to a central pole which usually is 'tensioned' between the ceiling and floor of a room. Natural materials were often used such as paper, rattan, raffia, bergère cane and shells. The most iconic of these are the multi-tiered shell chandeliers named 'FUN', designed by Verner Panton in the mid-60s. Although many replicated these designs, they are often referred to as Panton shell lights. The humble paper globe was also a stable design in 70s homes for its simplicity and inexpensive nature, popularized by Terence Conran through his Habitat store.

COLOURED BULBS

Don't overlook bulbs and how they can impact a design. Subtle changes in colour or even colour-changing projections can make an interesting talking point, especially at parties. If possible, test or think about the shade colour when lit. When I purchased my orange living room light online, I fell in love with it and didn't stop for one moment to think what colour the globes would glow... Yeah, you guessed it, ORANGE. Now, I love orange, but when your house glows like it's been attacked by aliens this can be a teeny-weeny bit of a problem, especially if you are eating, and everything, and I mean EVERYTHING, is basked in a lovely orange glow... Our home is a glowing beacon of orange in the evenings; if that is for you, cool, but forewarned is forearmed as they say.

ROCKET LAMPS

Another lamp, ubiquitous in British homes of the period is the 'rocket' lamp. Simply and inexpensively made from a tube of fibreglass and attached to three shaped teak legs, these have retained popularity as a mainstay of 70s lighting and are highly desired. Their value is determined by the quality, not only of the spindly teak legs which are prone to breaking, but the fibreglass shade which can degrade and crack over time.

Lava lamps

Pulsating, globules of wax, seemingly dancing, and held in a coloured liquid... Lava lamps, so called because of their lava-like wax, are unique in the fact that they are less about creating actual light and more about creating an ambience perfect for the acid-soaked culture of the 60s and 70s.

The love affair with the lava lamp was still alive in the 70s, despite the light being invented and popularized in the 60s. Some may say that its appeal and classic design is still as relevant today as it was over 60 years ago, remaining a firm fixture in many people's homes. The 'Astro' lamp, as it was first called when it was launched in 1963 by eccentric inventor (and naturist) Edward Craven Walker, was an instant success and has had lasting popularity since, still appearing in lists of iconic design classics.

The first lamps were developed using household objects such as glass cocktail shakers and squash bottles, until the quintessential shape that we know and love today was developed. This has proved such an enduring classic that it has never been out of production. It has appeared countless times in the media

and famous owners include Ringo Starr and David Bowie – the latter had a miniature version in his recording studio.

I first became aware of the lava lamp in the early 90s as a teen, when I saved up my pennies to pay the £54 ($65) to light up my bedroom. One of the things I adore, not only because of the recognizable design of the lamp, is the fact that during the 50-plus years they have been in production, Crestworth (later Mathmos) lava lamps have been made solely in the UK, from the glass bottles blown in Yorkshire, to the filling, which is still done from their headquarters in Poole, Dorset. Another amazing fact is that all their lamps are recyclable, with replacement bottles, fittings and bulbs, going right back to the 60s, so you can keep your precious lamp going indefinitely – the perfect sustainable lamp. Although the exact recipe is a closely guarded secret, the principle of the lamp is deceptively simple, changing very little since the early days of production. The globules are actually a form of wax inside a sealed unit of liquid; the glass section has a metal coil at the base of the lamp which rests on top of a bulb, this heats the wax so that it melts, becoming less dense than the liquid, which enables it to float towards the top of the lamp. As the wax reaches the top, it cools just enough for it to harden slightly and sink and the cycle continues perpetually.

Vintage lava lamps are incredibly collectable and were

Interesting fact

The use of lava lamps helps protect our internet security. Cybersecurity firm Cloudflare uses over 100 pulsing lava lamps to create random patterns to generate code to prevent hackers from accessing data.

issued in many designs and colourways. Crestworth produced varying designs, including the more traditional 'Astro' lantern, based on a hurricane lamp; the slightly steampunk-esque 'Traction Engine' lamp; and the 'Nordic', which was a high-end design favoured in executive clubs.

Crestworth also produced a range of space-age fibre-optic lamps, the lesser known 'Phantom Lite' in 1973, the forerunner of the 1975 'Galaxy', in which thousands of colour-changing fibre-optic strands are encased in a dark and futuristic plastic dome, and the 'Glitter Lite', a similar premise to the lava lamp, but guess what, in glitter.

Caring for your lava lamp

✸ Keep the lamp away from direct sunlight as this affects the wax and the colours of the lamp.
✸ For best results keep at room temperature.
✸ Always use the recommended bulb.
✸ Do not move, drop or shake the glass bottle while it is warm.
✸ Do not remove the cap of the glass bottle.
✸ Give the light enough time to warm up, this can be anything over 2 hours.
✸ A cloudy lava lamp is often the result of shaking the glass while warm, if this happens, switch off and let the wax harden, preferably overnight at room temperature. Turn the light on just enough to soften the wax, but not to move, then shut it off again overnight and then let it run for over 8 hours. If the light has one large blob at the bottom, the metal coil may be dislodged, or you might be using an incorrect bulb.

Tips for buying

✸ You can buy a new modern Mathmos lamp for a reasonable proce, made to exactly the same design as the original. These are guaranteed to work, be safe and look great in your home.
✸ Original 60s and 70s lamps, including the fibre-optic models, will always be strong with avid collectors with prices ranging from the low hundreds for a lava lamp and upwards for a nice example of a 'Galaxy'.
✸ As with all electricals, ensure these are PAT-tested before use to ensure that they are safe for the modern home.

Shag pile

David Hockney painting *Mr and Mrs Clark and Percy*, featuring 70s it-couple fashion designer Ossie Clark and his wife, textile designer Celia Birtwell.

Along with flokati, Scandinavian rugs were also a popular choice due to the wealth of colours and designs. Often referred to as 'rya' rugs, these rugs were typical across Scandinavia, where they were traditionally used, not on the floor, but as bed covers during the long winter nights. By the early 60s Danish carpet-producer Ege Rya made rya rugs, using industrial machines rather than knotting by hand. These rugs were sold as 100 per cent wool with a 2.5cm (1in) pile with colour and moth proofing and guaranteed for 25 years. The continued love of all things Scandinavian throughout the decade, combined with far-out colours and designs, meant that rya rugs were a sure-fire hit for the hip and trendy.

During the 70s you couldn't say that you had a contemporary interior design scheme unless you had something shaggy, paired with the orange-hued teak woods, smoked glass and chrome. Shag brought colour, texture and warmth into an interior. These often-psychedelic rugs were in the decade's most popular colours of avocado green, harvest yellow, rust orange, royal purple and turd brown.

One of my favourite examples I own is the large, circular design, by British company Axminster, which has a long, illustrious carpet-making heritage since 1755. During the late 60s and throughout the 70s they caught onto the trend for shag rugs and

Shag, although it should have never left, is back and more desirable than Burt Reynolds (on a shag carpet in *Cosmopolitan*).

One of the most enduring images of the 70s, shag rugs and carpets are perfect for lolling about on listening to music, watching TV and losing small things in – like earrings, Lego and occasionally breakfast cereal. It was incredibly popular either to have rugs or to carpet your whole house (and walls, if you were Jayne Mansfield). Thankfully, today, the urge to cover your bathroom in it has waned. In the 70s the concept of wall-to-wall carpets was only a few decades old and the urge to experiment with manufacturing techniques, fabrics and colours was high. Although these wall-to-wall carpets, popularized in the US by *The Brady Bunch*, are oozing in 70s style, their origins are much humbler.

Shag pile rugs can be traced back to the use of flokati rugs in Ancient Greece, made from hand-woven sheep fleece or goat hair. Former First Lady Jackie Kennedy Onassis was partly responsible for the popularity of flokati in the early 70s when she married multi-millionaire Aristotle Onassis, and decorated their home on the Greek island of Skorpios. You can also see a flokati rug on the floor of the started producing a range under the 'Axminster Norsk' label, borrowing heavily from Scandinavian traditions. My parents originally bought this rug when they lived in London in 1969 or early 1970 and it was placed in the centre of their living room in their first flat in Fulham, which they rented from my father's firm. The newly married 22-year-olds paired this bright rug with a chrome and glass circular coffee table, dark green curtains and orange walls. The quality of the rug stands testament to the number of years my parents owned it, as it survived three house moves and a flood. Its final resting place was my bedroom, once it was a little threadbare and with bits of Play-Doh stuck to it. One day, in the early 1990s my parents decided to burn the rug to finally make way for something new. That rug was one of my most enduring memories of my childhood; playing on its brightly patterned designs, running my fingers through the long pile and watching *The Muppet Show*.

I searched for that rug in the formative days of eBay and occasionally saw them, some in poor condition; some too expensive for my limited budget; and some removed from sale before the auction finished. I felt that 'my' rug would remain elusive, until 2019, when I started following the Instagram page @dogwoodlifestyle. Natalie, the owner, had my rug! I told her the story of how much this rug meant to me, and we became firm friends, bonding over similar interests. One day, she turned up on my doorstep with the rug in hand, gifting it to me. Natalie will tell you: 'The day I swapped my rug for a best friend was the best deal I've ever done'.

For your own modern interior, rugs are a really undervalued way of decorating. A bright, shaggy rug brings a textural quality to the room, and isn't a big commitment in terms of design. It is simple to roll up and move; it's like choosing art, for the floor.

Retired Ege director J. Vagn Larsen estimates that more than a million ryas were sold globally during the late 60s and throughout the 70s – the golden years of shag pile. Larger rugs were expensive to produce and retail at the time so smaller rugs were introduced to be used on floors or as wall hangings. As a result these survive in greater numbers, pushing up the value of larger, statement carpets in the modern-day market, but by the 80s they were no longer in vogue.

Today rya style rugs have not faded with the passing of time in either colour or desirability. On the contrary, in recent years their prices have sky rocketed as collectors and enthusiasts search to buy the biggest and best examples. A good vintage rug should be considered an investment piece, much like art. Examples from Ege, Axminster and Dutch brand Desso, which made huge rugs in polyacryl wool can still be found. Prices vary depending on design, colour, size and desirability, but they often start at £250 ($300) if you are lucky enough. High-end pieces from designers such as Verner Panton's 'Mira-X' collection can fetch upwards of £5,000 ($5,700) for a smaller example. Cost-effective alternatives include homemade latchwork kits, popular from the 50s to the 70s, for people to craft their own rugs.

BELOW, ME AND MY YOUNGER SISTER IN 1980, SITTING ON THE ORIGINAL AXMINSTER RUG.

Care for your rug

* Flea spray – You don't want any extra visitors to the house.
* Moth treatment – If it is a smaller piece, you can pop it in a cotton bag and put it in the deep freeze for a week or so to kill any larvae.
* Check for stains and marks and spot clean with a spray or foam cleaner.
* Vacuum thoroughly. If small enough, I shake and beat it first to dislodge deep down dirt as the long pile tends to hide crumbs and debris.
* You can clean short pile vintage rugs using a professional carpet cleaner you can hire from hardware stores, but I urge you to err on the side of caution with long/thick shag pile rugs as these hold lot of water weight and struggle to dry naturally. The long pile is not suitable for the rotary action of the cleaner. I have had some success with the upholstery tool, but would recommend that this is undertaken in summer, especially for larger pieces that can be hung out to dry outside.
* If you can, rotate the rug frequently to ensure that it wears evenly in high-traffic areas.
* As tempting as it is to clean smaller handmade rugs by popping them into a washing machine, they rarely survive the process (much to my own chagrin and experience). It would be best to remove as much dust as possible by vacuuming and beating and then spot cleaning where possible.

How to buy a rug

* Be aware that larger, brighter rugs will be costly.
* Buying in person is recommended as you can see (and smell) the rug. Experienced sellers often have items professionally cleaned before sale, which will increase their cost. However, with some time and effort, a cheaper, uncleaned item could be a bargain.
* Check for any nasty whiffs, including pet accidents, damp/mould smells and marks from years of storage which could be difficult to remove.
* Check for stains. Some can be easily removed with household cleaners but large, ground-in stains could be costly.
* Check to see if there is any missing thread or bald pile. Small amounts of wear are to be expected but large holes and missing threads are bad news.
* When buying online it is difficult to establish the rug's condition. Zooming in on photos helps, but it is often a gamble. I have bought rugs that look grim from photos and have turned out to be in great condition, and vice versa.

Art

Such was the variance in interior styles across the decade that it is hard to pinpoint trends of art which dominated the period as in other eras. Homespun art kits competed with mass-market raunchy lady classics, and op art was still popular into the early to mid-70s, giving a modern space-age feel. There is no overall style that sets the decade apart, it is such a rich and interesting subject to see the huge stylistic differences, most of which I could never hope to be able to cover in a book this size. I have therefore given you an entry-level taster into some popular styles of the era which you can explore further.

ABOVE, ABSTRACT OIL PAINTINGS IN TONAL COLOURS SIT BESIDE A BOLD, GRAPHIC DESERT IMAGE, REMINISCENT OF PAINTING BY NUMBERS – A POPULAR PASTIME IN THE HOME OF LAURA @SAVAGEHOUSE1970. RIGHT, ELSEWHERE IN THE HOME THIS EYE-CATCHING HIROSHI AWATSUJI DESIGN ABOVE THE VINTAGE PLAYPEN COUCH PROVES THAT LESS IS IN FACT MORE WHEN CURATING A STYLISH HOME.
PAGE 145, THE DINING ROOM OF LAURA @SAVAGEHOUSE1970, FEATURING A FLOKATI RUG AND A CHARMING UBIQUITOUS MACRAMÉ OWL.

MICHAEL ENGLISH

This British artist is one of my favourites and was known for designing poster in the 60s for esteemed musicians such as Jimi Hendrix. He collaborated with Nigel Waymouth of the 60s boutique Granny Takes a Trip, and they established a design company called Hapshash and the Coloured Coat which designed psychedelic posters in the 60s. One of these was the Pink Floyd poster UFO club 67 in pink and orange, which we are lucky enough to have a copy of, signed by Nigel Waymouth. By the late 60s and early 70s, English moved away from the psychedelic imagery of the 60s and moved towards hyperrealism with the use of an airbrush. There are several collections of this work, which can be found in interior design books of the period. *The Food Series* (1969–70) and *Rubbish Posters* (1970) both included pop art sensibilities featuring household items such as ketchup bottles and Coca-Cola bottle caps.

ATHENA

Founded in 1964 in Hampstead, London, by Ole Christensen, this British retail chain sold mass-produced iconic posters. The company and its resulting success caused art critics to denounce the shop, claiming the posters were too vulgar to be considered art. Most famous of these is the *Tennis Girl* poster of a female tennis player, *sans* undies, which has become a pop icon. Another was the famous 1976 *Lord of the Rings* poster which was illustrated by 17-year-old Jimmy Cauty, who is better known for being one half of the musical duo The KLF, one of the 90s' most successful musical groups, and co-founder of British electronic music group The Orb.

OP ART

This uber graphic movement emerged in the 60s and went mainstream in the 70s. A form of abstract art, it gives the illusion of movement by the clever use of pattern and colour. Hungarian-French artist Victor Vasarely is widely regarded as the grandfather of op art, with his earliest pieces dating to the 30s. English artist Bridget Riley is also cited as one of the most important artists in the genre. Letterman is a popular name, especially in the US, where artworks were sold during the 70s through the chain JCPenney. These paintings, often triptychs featuring everything from simple landscapes to geometric patterns, are highly collectable for their 70s aesthetic. There is no one Letterman artist, these pieces were produced en masse to hang in any average home.

Greg Copeland is another studio name to look out for, again mostly in the US. The studio employs many artists, who are famous for their silkscreen mirror pieces.

MACRAMÉ

Originally dating back to thirteenth-century Arabia, macramé – the art of weaving and knotting jute or rope – had a massive explosion in the 70s as the craft of choice for many.

Whether it was partly the 'back to nature' hippie counter-culture of wanting more of a handmade aesthetic in homes (and wardrobes), people went crazy for it. Nothing sums up a decade more than a spider plant in a jute macramé hanger, or the ubiquitous macramé owl (why was it always an owl?) hanging on the wall.

Original pieces of macramé are harder to find; as with many daily objects they were simply discarded when no longer fashionable. The good news is that there are many macramé artists using traditional patterns to produce new pieces which are fairly inexpensive, and you get to support a local business too. Or, if you are feeling creative and crafty, there are lots of tutorials online where you can make your own plant hangers, wall hangings or even an owl.

WALL HANGINGS

Folk-art wall hangings were popular, made not only from macramé but also miniature latch hook rugs by German company Junghans Wolle.

Another popular crafting-activity-cum-home-decoration was crewel embroidery, available in kit form, stitching designs in wool using a technique that dates back hundreds of years, with some designs now highly collectable.

A third that became all the rage was 'string art', creating art from household items. Straight lines are formed by wrapping brightly coloured thread or wire around pins nailed into a fabric-covered board. The slightly different angles of the pins where the thread intersects give the appearance of Bezier curves (named after French engineer Pierre Bézier who used it to design curves for the bodywork of Renault cars in the 60s). Popular kits included geometric shapes, boats, butterflies and of course owls (always the owls). String art is visually similar to the geometric drawing device, which in 1965 was marketed as the creative toy Spirograph.

HOW I CREATED

STATEMENT ART

I much prefer a huge statement piece of art than lots of small pieces. You can create your own large, impactful statement art by stretching vintage fabric onto canvas frames. This easy-to-do craft gives you large, graphic and period correct art for your home on a relatively small budget. This is something that we do in our home to create large works of art which can otherwise be prohibitively expensive.

What you will need:
Staple gun
Staples
Canvas frame – available on eBay
Hammer to assemble the frame
   (the frame comes with easily
    assembled joints)
Fabric of your choice

Measure your fabric and purchase the appropriately sized canvas frame. Prepare the fabric by ironing any creases; place the fabric on a hard surface (I use the floor) face down and arrange the wood frame on the reverse of the fabric. Pull the top edge of the fabric over the wood baton and staple, do the same with the opposite side, and repeat at the other two sides. Ensure that the fabric is pulled tight but not over stretched. Work your way around the wood, pulling the fabric gently and stapling as you go, taking care not to stretch and distort the fabric.

Making use of what you have

The best pieces may be something you already own! One of the easiest solutions to making something work in your new retro pad is to make something ordinary look extraordinary with the clever use of paint, vinyl and possibly a change of handle.

Some of my favourite pieces of furniture that are in daily use are ones where I have tweaked their looks so that they are more in keeping with the house. One of these success stories was the kitchen makeover (see page 90) and another is the office, where I used mainly IKEA furniture and vinyl to give a more pleasing retro vibe. Each of the pieces in the office were found on Facebook marketplace and the furniture of the whole room came to less than £175 ($200). My favourite upcycles are the tulip base from IKEA 'Docksta' table where I placed a new piece of MDF covered with vinyl to make a workable desk area. The shelving was a 1980s mock-Georgian Ladderax which I bought for £20 ($25) and was advertised as 'shelves'. The ladders were badly damaged, and the dark mahogany colour didn't work for me so some paint and vinyl turned them into something that I could use. I don't usually advocate painting mid-century or vintage furniture, but if pieces are badly damaged and destined for the dump then it's worth having a little experiment with them.

Not all projects have to be large; something simple like covering the front of a basic plastic laminate chest of drawers with some cheerful retro vinyl can really make a statement out of what would ordinarily be a dull piece of furniture.

Why buy vintage?

The problem with fast fashion, and the damage it is doing to our environment, is well-known. However, more insidious and possibly far more damaging is the notion of fast interiors. We don't hear about this so much, simply because it is not as prevalent in the media and so people still have an 'out of sight, out of mind' mentality when it comes to disposing of unwanted items. It is hard to get exact figures and it is suspected that this is grossly underestimated, but more than 20 million pieces of furniture and accessories are disposed of each year. Out of this, only a tiny percentage is recycled because mixed materials cannot economically be separated for recycling.

As with fast fashion, the environmental issues of fast furniture are closely tied to ethical ones. Where once the manufacturing of items was domestic and one of pride and craftmanship, it has now been transferred offshore to lower the manufacturing costs. However, there is still a cost; not only is the planet being exploited for natural resources, but people's health is at risk with the amount of chemicals now used in modern mass-production methods. Even more interesting is that many of these companies reference vintage pieces as inspiration for their designs.

This disposable nature of furniture results in part from the rise in the number of people renting rather than buying homes, because it is easier to buy something new and cheap from the high street or online rather than pay to move items to new properties. The linear nature of consumerism – constantly buying new things then dumping them – is incredibly wasteful and it's encouraged by social media.

That is not to say that nobody can ever purchase anything new ever again. Considered purchases where you have a genuine need or love for the item which you can cherish for years to come are always welcomed. However, does the world really need another resin pineapple which you throw in your shopping trolley as an afterthought then throw away six months later as it doesn't go with your aesthetic? There are also a whole host of independent creative people trying to forge another way – one of producing on a bespoke basis direct for the customer – so that excess and unpurchased stock doesn't end up in landfill when it doesn't sell. People are using reclaimed materials from leather for shoes, fabrics for home accessories or simply choosing to sell vintage to earn their crust. These independent businesses offer a unique customer service that usually goes above and beyond, as well as with individual items not seen elsewhere.

The profits of independent businesses go directly into their business and support their livelihoods, as well as those of local suppliers, rather than lining the pockets of fat-cat corporations.

RIGHT, SPECIALIST DEALERS WILL BE ABLE TO GIVE YOU ADVICE ON BUYING PIECES FOR YOUR HOME. THEY WILL ALSO HAVE DONE ALL THE HARD WORK RENOVATING PIECES FOR YOU AND WILL OFTEN DELIVER DIRECT TO YOU.

So why buy vintage?

Some of the negative comments I have had over the years come from the misconception that buying second-hand furniture, clothing and accessories is somehow less; that you can't afford to buy new, in a snobbish way that makes you feel like you aren't succeeding in life. I'm here to dispel that myth.

I say: 'Second-hand doesn't have to mean second rate'.

Mostly people ask: Doesn't it smell? It's gross buying other people's cast offs; I'll get fleas! It's dirty, it's a dead person's thing... Showing pictures of my home and others' in this book hopefully reveal that none of this is true. On the contrary, when buying vintage or second-hand you are usually getting something very well made for less money than a high-street replica, one that will have a shelf life of longer than five years and that will appreciate in value. Over the years I have upgraded my furniture, selling one piece to fund another, and if I had bought high street, I would have lost money on these pieces and would have struggled to sell them for a fifth of their original value.

Doesn't it smell?

On the whole, no. Well-loved and cherished pieces often smell of delicious furniture wax, or of the natural wood, at worst a little fusty from storage. That, however, is not to say that I haven't bought the odd stinker in my time, from the era of chain smoking it is likely that some things will need a good clean and air.

If the thought of hard graft in cleaning a piece of vintage furniture puts you off then there are many reputable vintage dealers specializing in mid-century and 70s furniture who will do the hard graft for you; however, you will pay for their services with a higher retail price. If it's a bargain you're after then you're best looking for something that needs a bit of tender loving care that you can spruce up yourself with items you often have around the house. Bicarbonate of soda is wonderful for getting rid of nasty niffs, but most often or not a good airing and some sunlight will kill off most smells, especially in clothing or soft furnishings that cannot be easily laundered.

ABOVE, DON'T BE PUT OFF BUYING A SECOND-HAND CHAIR THAT HAS SEEN BETTER DAYS, A TRUSTED UPHOLSTERER WILL BE ABLE TO TRANSFORM A TIRED PIECE INTO SOMETHING SHOWSTOPPING AND YOU WILL BE INVESTING IN THEIR SKILLS AND CRAFT – AND SUPPORTING A SMALL BUSINESS TO BOOT.

WHERE TO BUY VINTAGE?

It is much easier to buy vintage now than it used to be 20 or even ten years ago. There are so many specialists who are generous with their knowledge if you want something specific, or even if you don't know what you are looking for, they will be able to help you with their years of experience. This is the main benefit of purchasing from a specialist dealer. Once upon a time you could pick items up from junk shops and jumble sales, but these are not as common as they once were. The former, mostly house clearances, used to be a treasure trove of tat and I used to love a good rummage. These were the places that you found items from the 60s and 70s, with antiques shops of the time not catering to mid-century and the sexy term of vintage not being in common use.

Now it is all mostly online; the reduction of overheads means that many house clearances no longer have to rely on bricks and mortar shops for trade. There are now more specialist shops which cater to this growing market, as well as vintage emporiums which house multiple dealers within one building. Here are the best places I have found to buy vintage pieces for your home:

Local auctions

Local auctions still turn up gems, especially from people working with house clearances or solicitors working with probate. Subscribe to their catalogues; most allow you to bid online, and some still have viewing days where you can look before you place a bid. Remember, there will be tax added to your purchasing bid and sometimes additional fees, which will be listed for you to be made aware of before you purchase.

Attending an auction is very exciting and high-octane, where you can see people bidding against you. It is tempting to overbid when you are caught up in the moment, so it is useful to have in mind a price you wish to pay, plus any fees, before you bid so that you don't get carried away.

Antiques markets/Festivals

Treat these very much like the other events listed above. Arrive early, wear comfy shoes, take lots of cash. However, these will be specialist traders dealing so will usually take credit or debit cards for larger purchases. You will also have much better quality, restored and curated items for sale which will result in higher prices. Prices at events such as these still tend to be slightly more reduced than in specialist bricks and mortar shops.

Etsy

The home of crafts and vintage. There are lots of sellers on this platform, which is great for all sorts of items. Again, use broad search words to find interesting things. Items on Etsy are likely to be priced slightly on the higher side to cover Etsy fees and to offer free delivery. Have a look to see if the seller has a personal website where you can often buy direct at a reduced price.

Facebook Marketplace/ Craigslist/Gumtree

It may take some trawling through a lot of random items, but often you find treasures buried deep. These sites are especially good for large items such as sofas and dining tables as well as sideboards, and people usually want these larger items collected ASAP. Be aware that desirable items often go very quickly, especially if they are priced reasonably. It is best to be able to collect the item very swiftly, sometimes same day, so that your beloved bargain doesn't go to another buyer. You can search for anything you want and set your location parameters as to how far you wish to travel. Remember to take the cash with you and ask to see the item when you collect to make sure that you are getting what you wanted.

Charity shops/ Thrift stores

In the UK, charity shops, where people donate unwanted items, are very common. Similar to thrift stores elsewhere in the world, they offer a chance to buy used and quality items at a reduced rate. Charity shops were a rich seam of items 20 years ago, but as the years have passed, quality donations are now often auctioned by the charity directly through eBay to get the most money. It is rare that I find a really good bargain in these shops any more as they are mostly filled with fast fashion items. There are a few exceptions where charity shops have seen a niche in the market and have shops especially dedicated only to vintage items.

Thrift stores in the US in particular seem to be larger and have more of a varied amount of stock to choose from compared to their UK counterparts.

Car boot sales

Where other countries have estate sales to clear people's homes of unwanted items, the UK has something called a car boot sale. This is a peculiarly British pastime of filling your car with unwanted items, driving to a field and unloading it all onto a pasting table for strangers to wander past and purchase. These are similar to flea markets but usually are just members of the general public rather than dealers or traders. They are usually organized at weekends, start early, and are possibly the most fun you can have with usually very little cash. They are absolutely, hands down, my favourite way to spend an early morning – rummaging in someone else's trash surrounded by a field which may or may not be covered in animal poo (I'll come to that in a moment). Turn over for my top tips for navigating car boot sales.

Car boot sale
Top Tips

* Get there early. The early bird catches the worm as they say, and dealers will be sniffing around first thing to get bargains so get yourself there too for a chance to find the best stuff.

* Have a cross-body bag to protect your valuables. I take lots of change in small waist bag. DO take lots of change, as the sellers won't take credit cards!

* Don't go in your finest vintage. The sellers will spot what you like a mile off and may raise the prices. Personally I usually go looking like I've slept in a hedge the night before; I don't even wash my hair or put make up on. I'm not even sure that stealth tactic works, but who wants to put mascara on at 6am to walk around a damp field?

* Talking of damp fields, these are often farmers' properties and livestock have usually been grazing the day before. Expect the worst, and don't wear fancy shoes that will get trashed. Wear something comfortable and that you don't mind getting dirty in case you happen to tread in something a bit nasty.

* Take a snack, drink and sun cream in the summer. Maybe also take a hat and sunglasses, as it can be hot work out there. Take a granny trolley, or failing that, lots of bags for your bargains.

* Do look under tables and in boxes, as that is where the treasure lies – go forage! Do haggle, but don't be rude. You'll catch more flies with honey than vinegar as the saying goes – you are more likely to grab a bargain if you are kind and respectful. Always remember your manners and start by offering one-third lower. Don't offer 20p ($0.20) for a £2 ($2) item; no one wants to be THAT person. You'll more likely get a deal if you buy lots of items from one person.

* Act cool; pretend you don't know what something is, even if your entire body is screaming for joy, keep that poker face!

* Don't be afraid to walk away if the price isn't the one you want to pay. Have a walk around and come back and offer again before you leave, you may be able to secure a better deal if no one else has wanted to buy the item. HOWEVER, nothing haunts you like the vintage you DIDN'T buy, so don't be mean if the price is fair and you really want it.

* If you're late to the event, don't sweat it, some of my best bargains have been at the end of the day when people reduce the price of items so that they don't have to take them home again.

* Buy with your gut instinct. I cannot stress this enough. If you like the look of something and you have no clue what it is or whether it might be worth £1,000 ($1,300) or 50p ($0.50), buy it. I've bought some right clangers in my time, thinking they were something they weren't, but I've also bought random items for very little which have turned out to be valuable. By the way, sometimes even the clangers can be worth something to you emotionally, as I always say, buy something YOU LOVE.

eBay

I was an early adopter of eBay, pre-PayPal when you wrote cheques to people and waited for your goods to arrive in the post – imagine! One of the first items I 'won' was an unopened tin of Biba baked beans from the Big Biba era. I owned these for nearly 15 years before they succumbed to rust, resulting in a 50-year-old tomato sauce explosion, so that I had decomposed bean and rust sludge across my kitchen.

Some of my best buys have been on this website, and the feeling of winning an auction with the palpitations of fear and excitement in your chest for a hard-won bidding war will never tire. Two notable purchases was our Ladderax unit and living room lights, both of which I had shipped from Italy at the time. With lots of couriers available, don't limit yourself to local items.

You can bid on an auction, make offers, or buy items instantly – it depends how the seller wishes to list these. Be aware of eBay's rules so that you don't get blacklisted. Unlike auction houses, the price you see, plus delivery, is the price you pay. The seller forfeits the fees on auction sites such as this.

eBay Top Tips

✱ Use different spellings or random general search words rather than specific items, as it is likely to bring up more interesting items within your budget. Rather than 'G Plan sideboard', try 'retro sideboard'; you might have to scroll through more items but you might just find a bargain.

✱ Modern etiquette: don't share cool items on social media that you aren't, or even are, bidding on. Someone could be quite annoyed if they're waiting for an item's auction to end at under a pound and there's a sudden influx of bidders!

Is it OK to mix vintage and modern in my home?

Absolutely! One of the things I always tell people is to buy what you LOVE. If you really love a piece then it says something about you, and your home should totally reflect you and your personality and passions. When walking into a home you should always be able to tell something about the person who lives there. Buying into trends and fashions only to ditch the items a year later is far more damaging to the environment than buying a few cherished pieces that you will keep for years.

To curate a collection takes time… years, decades even; mine has almost been my life's work. There are no hard and fast rules when it comes to decorating and furnishing your home – it should be an expression of you.

AT HOME WITH
@70sHOUSE MANCHESTER

"Fashion changes, but style endures." COCO CHANEL

Fashion

Fashion was always my first love. From a very early age I would pore over historical fashion books, looking at Victorian crinolines and bustles, Edwardian hobble skirts, the glamour of old Hollywood with bias-cut satin, post-war fashions from 60s 'Mod' looks to 70s hippie styles of long flowing skirts. I would hunt down clothing in second-hand and charity shops where supply was bountiful and get my mum to crochet pieces for me. Throughout my school years I was heavily influenced by 60s and 70s counter-culture, and dressed accordingly, much to the mirth of my peers. Music and clothing were everything during my young teens, before I started collecting larger pieces of furniture in my late teens and twenties. It is no surprise that I ended up studying fashion design at university, then later, working in the fashion industry for over 20 years.

Today, I still love buying and sourcing vintage clothing, especially glamorous eveningwear from the 70s which I usually sport while filming *The Bidding Room*. Daily, I am usually looking after our child or doing DIY which means I don't wear it most days. However, up until six years ago I wore vintage clothing to work on an almost daily basis, with a magpie eye for bright colours and patterns, similar to my taste in interiors.

It is much easier to find good-quality vintage clothing these days; there is a wealth of specialist bricks and mortar shops as well as online shops and sellers specializing in different eras. You can still occasionally find gems in charity shops, but this is usually few and far between unless they have a specialist section.

Some items of clothing are particularly difficult to get hold of, especially jeans and everyday clothes and shoes, but luckily there are plenty of ethical, slow-fashion brands to cater for those that want the look but cannot find or afford the originals. Brands such as The Hippie Shake, L'Atelier de Charlotte, and Terry de Havilland in the UK, Miracle Eye, Classic Rock Couture and Big Bud Press in the US, and Nine Lives Bazaar in Australia.

When buying vintage clothing please remember that they are not brand-new items, they have lived a life previously and that is part of the charm. As with interior pieces, I like to think about their past and the lives the items have seen, who their owners were and what they did; this gives the pieces a history which intrigues me. As you are purchasing for your own personal style and not buying what is currently in fashion, you will make wiser purchases that will last you longer than disposable fast fashion. I have vintage pieces from the 60s and 70s that I still wear today that I purchased when I was in my teens in the late 90s!

TIPS FOR BUYING VINTAGE CLOTHING

* Don't get hung up on the size label. Vintage sizing is dramatically different from modern sizing. A modern UK 14 is approximately a vintage 18. Use your body measurements or measurements of a favourite piece of clothing that fits well to compare with.

* Don't be afraid to try something on that is out of your comfort zone. Sometimes outfits need to be worn to convey their true beauty.

* When vintage shopping, try items on if you can to check the fit; if not refer to your measurements.

* Items *may* smell. Some odours can be laundered out, and hanging clothing outside on a bright day will diffuse others. If the smell of old perfume or perspiration persists, I have had great success with white vinegar or sprays designed to clean up pet accidents as they target the enzymes that cause the smell.

* Most everyday items can be laundered, check the care label if the garment contains one. These were introduced in the mid-60s, but not widely used until the 70s.

* Check zips and buttons. These, however, can be replaced with vintage or modern ones if they are missing.

* Know the shapes and silhouettes of the era you are buying from, this will help you to identify modern copies from original pieces. While I have no problem with vintage-inspired designs, if you are paying a premium for a vintage dress then you want to know it is the real deal.
* Stains can be an issue, but sometimes these can wash out easily or be treated with specialist stain preparations for pen marks etc. Be mindful of this when purchasing, it could be worth the risk.
* Holes – moth damage and cigarette holes can be incredibly difficult to repair. Moth larvae love dirty clothes made from natural fibres, and it is they that do the damage, not the moths themselves. Always hold knitwear up to the light and check for tiny holes. Holding it up to the light will also show up fabric which maybe overtly worn and thin, or any repairs that the garment has had.
* Vintage garments tend to have larger seams, so check this if the garment is a little snug and don't instantly dismiss it, as many items can be altered to fit you by specialists. Beware of garments that need too many repairs or alterations; take a deep breath and know that something better will come along.

I may argue that the 70s wasn't the one that taste forgot in interiors, but culinary-wise it had some dubious moments. In fact, celebrated chef Heston Blumenthal declared it 'the decade that good food forgot'.

Women's Liberation didn't just change the role of women in society, but also radically transformed what appeared on the dining table. By the 70s, 40 per cent of women were working, leading to a rise in convenience food. The means of keeping food fresh had also improved with around a third of British households owning a deep freezer by the 70s, rising to half of all households in 1980. Companies such as Bejam (founded in 1968) started selling low-cost, frozen foods to families. Food producers also noticed this trend and started to sell more food which could be prepared instantly or quickly and sold bright and colourfully branded foodstuffs. Growing up during this period, I know that I and others of a similar age have deep fondness and nostalgic lust for some 70s delicacies, some of which are still with us, some of which have been gone forever. Mention the following to someone over the age of 40 and watch their eyes mist over. Angel Delight – a mousse-based dessert made from adding flavoured powder to milk – delighted children, and was available in banana, chocolate, butterscotch and strawberry flavours. Other highlights were a Vesta Curry or Chow Mein, which were packets of dehydrated 'matter' which turned into something delicious, if lacking in nutrition. So, the delicious thing might be an exaggeration, but I would still eat one now. Primula cheese, basically herby cheese in a

Entertaining

metal tube, which you'd whack on a celery stick if you wanted to be fancy! Findus pancakes (they will burn the roof of your mouth), teamed with frozen peas and instant Smash mashed potatoes (simply add boiling water). I still eat a fish finger sandwich now (on thick white bread with salted butter and salad cream), and let's not forget the Arctic roll – delicious vanilla ice cream wrapped in sponge! My other half still lusts after a Sara Lee black forest gateau, which basically shows how many ways you can fit cherry flavour into a cake. Fray Bentos pies, established in 1961, were hugely popular for their convenience (bake in the tin they come in); I have to confess to never having eaten one, but they are still available today, so someone, somewhere, is still buying them. Finally, the last word on exotic food from the decade – the humble chicken Kiev (Kyiv), which first appeared on these shores courtesy of Marks & Spencer in 1979. This was the first chilled ready meal, opposed to frozen meal and was advertised as restaurant quality. They cost £1.99 (equivalent to over £9 [$10] in today's money), and flew off the shelves making ready meals a respectable alternative to home cooking. In direct conflict to this rise in processed food, you had a burgeoning community of people into what were termed 'health foods'. Even our tiny provincial town had 'The Health Food Shop' (yes, it was even called this), where you could procure lentils and other exotic food stuffs. They always smelled the same, a heady aroma of aniseed and dust. A modern 'superfood' that we take for granted appeared on the shores of the UK in the early 60s, but didn't take off until the swanky dinner parties of the 70s. Not just a bathroom colour, avacado was an exotic food which no one quite knew what to do with. Sold as avocado pears, people misunderstood and tried to bite through the tough skin, so special information was placed next to them to prevent customers from confusing them with fruit pears.

Television chefs had been steadily on the rise since the 50s, educating housewives of the day on how to cook. The very dependable Delia Smith, now a national treasure, cut her teeth on Anglia television in the 70s, showing us the basics. A quick search on the internet and you can find vintage videos of not only Delia, but also the dapper Graham Kerr, aka The Galloping Gourmet, whose boyish good looks and witty banter of double entendres, along with exquisite dress sense, was extremely popular. He claims to have invented the banana split and earned himself the dubious title of 'Liberace of the world food' by American food writer and critic Michael Field.

The other famous television cook, the bon viveur herself, was Fanny Cradock. Now I urge you, dear reader, if you have not previously heard of Fanny Cradock that you immediately look her up on YouTube, as seeing is indeed believing… Fanny, a terrifying matriarch, taught cookery alongside her henpecked husband Major Johnnie Cradock, whom she married bigamously. Fanny was as insane as she was vicious and the older she got, the higher the eyebrows and the more elaborate the evening dresses became, preferring to cook in pink chiffon rather than wear an apron. To typify Fanny's cooking would be like trying to bring the exotic to the average 60s and 70s housewife. She had a love of French cookery, and a fondness for green food-coloured mashed potatoes piped expertly around a dish. Her overblown style, 'above all, garnish and presentation', was all about impressing your neighbours who you didn't really like that much. To dub her an awful cook would be unfair; she introduced a version of pizza to the UK and claims to have invented prawn cocktail (although some argue that this can be traced as far back as French chef Auguste Escoffier). She was an excellent entrepreneur and business woman who promoted herself endlessly saying 'it's in the booklet', and who changed cookery programmes from dry educational television to full-on celebrity entertainment.

The 1975 Christmas series *Fanny Cradock cooks for Christmas* is one of the few full series left, and one which is repeated on the BBC in December. It is also available online and it is absolutely mesmerizing, well worth a watch if you have a spare hour to kill.

BIRTHDAY CAKES

Some of the most terrifying images in cookery books also happen to be children's cakes, from hedgehogs to crinoline ladies to clowns. My own mother was not known for her cake decorating prowess and each year successive arrays of troubling cakes would appear on our birthdays. We still discuss, through tears of laughter, my sixth birthday offering which was meant to be a carousel; she had in all honestly outdone herself with straws with painted horses and a wrapping paper canopy. That was until she lit the candles and she could see that something was going very wrong. There were urgent cries to 'blow the bloody candles out' as the entire canopy caught fire and went up in flames. My sister and I and a gaggle of six-year-olds stood agog at my father running through the village hall with a cake that looked like it was on the TV show *999: What's Your Emergency?* with the buttercream covered in bits of charred gift wrap…

Fun Fact

Avocados have been eaten in Mexico since at least 500 BCE. The Aztecs referred to them as *ahuacatl*, a word they may have also used for testicle which understandably made the dish hard to market. They were also known in the US as alligator pears where the word avocado was not adopted until the 60s.

Prawn Cocktail

Prawn Cocktail

Add some Las Vegas glitz to your dinner party with this traditional seafood cocktail.

Handful of lettuce, shredded
1 tomato, thinly sliced
Handful of cooked prawns
Lemon wedge (to garnish)
Mix the following together for Marie Rose Sauce
2 tbsp tomato ketchup
2 tbsp mayonnaise or salad cream
Dash of Worcestershire sauce
Dash of brandy (optional)
Cayenne pepper, to taste

1. Add shredded lettuce to a suitable glass cocktail glass. Add thin slices of tomato at the sides of the glass.
2. Place prawns decoratively over the top, ensure that these are fully defrosted.
3. Drizzle the pre-prepared Marie Rose sauce over the top. Decorate with a wedge of lemon and serve with a smile.

Tequila Sunrise

Mick Jagger's favourite 1972 tour beverage is best served in a chilled, tall, slimline glass.

50ml/2fl oz tequila
100ml/3½fl oz fresh orange juice
Cup of ice, lightly crushed
1 tsp grenadine
Orange wedge and maraschino cherry, to garnish

1. Shake together tequila and orange juice.
Fill a glass with crushed ice cubes; pour in orange juice mixture.
2. Slowly pour in the grenadine, and allow it to settle to the bottom of the glass (be patient).
3. Garnish with a slice of orange, and a maraschino cherry on a cocktail umbrella and add a plastic monkey and a sparkler for true pizzazz.

Hedgehog Cake

Cheese Fondue

Molten cheese, with a hint of garlic and wine, how did this dish ever go out of fashion? Throwing keys into a bowl afterwards is optional.

1 clove garlic
300ml/½ pint white wine
1 tsp lemon juice
225g/8oz Emmental cheese, grated
225g/8oz Gruyère cheese, grated
1 tsp kirsch (optional)
1 tsp cornflour
Bread and pickles for dipping

1. Vigorously rub the cut halves of a clove of garlic into a fondue pot (or saucepan).
2. Add the white wine and lemon juice and heat until boiling. Lower the heat and stir in the grated cheese mix gradually until the cheese has completely melted in to the wine mix, stirring continuously.
3. If using, mix kirsch in a small cup with cornflour (use 1 tsp of water if not). Add this to the cheese mix and stir until smooth, do not allow to boil as it will burn.
4. Serve with bread and pickles for dipping.
5. Thank me later while you are in a cheese-induced coma.

eese Fondue

Banana Candle

The *70s House* adaptation of the famous Fanny Cradock recipe for children*.

1 banana – the straighter the better
Can of pineapple rings in juice
Strawberry jam
Finely chopped peanuts
4 maraschino or glacé cherries
Vanilla custard for the candle wax

1. Place 2 pineapple rings in each dessert dish.
2. Unpeel the banana and cut the end straight, lightly brush the banana with warmed strawberry jam and roll in the chopped peanuts until covered.
3. Place this within the centre hole of the pineapple, ensure that there is a snug fit to avoid a flaccid dessert.
4. Carefully attach the cherry with a cocktail stick to the top of the banana, trying not to wince while doing so.
5. For authenticity, drizzle vanilla custard over the head of the fruit, letting it slowly run down the banana.
6. Serve with a knowing smile and bask in the praise of being the host with the most.
*Do not serve to children unless you want social services involved.

Drinks

We can't leave entertaining without talking about what drinks to serve. Lager was hugely popular in the 70s, with kegs such as Watney's Party 7 being sold for larger-scale gatherings. Other lager brands that you may have heard of, such as Skol or Carling (Black Label) are still sold today so you can imbibe in the flavours of the decade. Brands that have fallen by the wayside include Double Diamond, Worthington E and Harp.

Wines were being drunk, but the palate was quite different from what we consider today. People brought fancy bottles of straw-covered Chianti back from Italy, produced for the tourist market and sweet German wines, such as Blue Nun and Black Tower, and Mateus rosé wine from Portugal were being drunk. These wines are all still available to purchase, should you wish to. Another two small bottle drinks which are still available today are Cherry B and Goldwell Snowball, and you can also usually find matching vintage glasses to serve these in. Kitsch cocktails were also popular, the more garnish the better!

According to the cocktail bible, *Difford's Guide*, many cocktails that were popular in the 70s weren't necessarily created in the 70s, but enjoyed a resurgence, such as the Piña Colada, Harvey Wallbanger, Moscow Mule and Singapore Sling. The 70s bore a long line of sleezy-sounding cocktails including the Slow Screw and a Slow Comfortable Screw Against the Wall, when they adapted the popular Screwdriver cocktail. Others were named after popular films of the time like *The Godfather* (with tweaks such as the Godmother and The Boss); some retain a cult-like status: the Tequila Sunrise was so beloved by Mick Jagger that it fuelled the Rolling Stones' legendary 1972 tour across America, which was dubbed the 'Cocaine and Tequila Sunrise Tour' in Keith Richards' autobiography.

> **"She drank the Mateus rosé without even taking the lampshade off."** Victoria Wood

Estelle's Festive Fun Snowball

1 x double shot of Advocaat
1 x shot of ginger wine
Top up with good-quality lemonade. Stir and serve with a maraschino cherry on a cocktail umbrella.

Babycham

Another popular drink in the 70s, this fizzy perry (pear cider) is carefully packaged in cute little bottles that conveniently fill their own branded champagne-style coupe glasses, complete with dancing fawn. Marketed perfectly for ladies of the post-war era, when it was still deemed unladylike to drink a pint. Even if ladies did fancy a shandy (lager and lemonade) they would usually only drink half pints to appear sophisticated. Babycham was advertised on television, marketed as sophisticated and 'posh', with adverts showing raffish men and elegant ladies. It was a mainstay of alcoholic drinks from the 50s to the 70s. By the 80s, it was struggling with a reputation for being a bit naff. Babycham is still available today and is popular as a seasonal drink around Christmas. It is surprisingly drinkable and far nicer than the alcopops that it paved the way for.

Top Tip

Babycham glasses are often expensive, but how to tell the earlier, more valuable, from the later ones? Run your finger over the bottom of the bowl, where the stem joins, the older ones will have a pronounced bubble and the later, less desirable, ones will be completely flat.

SETTING THE MOOD

Some of the best-selling albums of the decade can be found in thrift shops, vintage shops, record fairs and online. The fact that they were best-selling means that they are in plentiful supply, but the prices are based on overall condition. The 70s were the golden age of the hi-fi, and almost all homes had a record player. After a time of falling out of favour for the vast majority in the 90s and 00s, vinyl is most definitely back and more sought-after than ever. So, what tunes should you be playing at your soirée? The following selection is based on some of the best-selling albums of the decade for your listening pleasure. This is not a decisive choice, but shows the range of tastes throughout the decade and is a useful reference point to start your own record collection.

SIMON & GARFUNKEL
1970
Bridge Over Troubled Water

PINK FLOYD
1973
The Dark Side of the Moon

STEVIE WONDER
1976
Songs in the Key of Life

FLEETWOOD MAC
1977
Rumours

LED ZEPPELIN
1971
IV

NEIL YOUNG
1972
Harvest

ELTON JOHN
1974
Greatest Hits

QUEEN
1975
A Night at the Opera

BLONDIE
1978
Parallel Lines

SUPERTRAMP
1979
Breakfast in America

One to watch
ABIGAIL'S PARTY

This evocative play for both stage and television, devised by British film director Mike Leigh in 1977, has endured as a staple of 70s iconography, from the clothes and the set design, to the satire of the aspirations and tastes of the new middle class which was emerging in Britain during the 70s. Initially running as a stage performance, it premiered in April 1977, and transmitted in November of the same year via the BBC's Play for Today series.

If you are not already aware of this classic piece of film, I urge you to watch it. The premise is that Beverly and her husband Laurence are holding a drinks party for their neighbours. The party starts off in a typically British stiff and formal way, until Beverly and Laurence start arguing and the more Beverly drinks, the more she overtly flirts with her neighbour's husband, culminating with Beverly proudly showing off her *Wings of Love* painting (see page 70). I promise you will never think of Demis Roussos the same again.....

Thank you, dear reader
I truly hope that you have enjoyed reading *70s House* as much as I enjoyed creating and writing about it. If this book has inspired you to create your own retro wonderland or given you the confidence to paint your living room bright orange, run your hands through a shag pile rug while listening to David Essex or to serve a Banana Candle at your next soirée, then my work here is done...

RESOURCES

70s House Manchester

www.70shousemanchester.com
@70shousemanchester
www.pateron.com/70shousemanchester

Shops

Apollo Retro www.apolloretro.com
Alfie Retro Robot @alfie_robot_retro
Atomic Drinkware www.atomicdrinkware.com
Balmer and Stanley Vintage @balmerandstanley
Biba Boys www.bibaboys.co.uk
Blue Lizard Textiles www.etsy.com/shop/bluelizardtextiles/
Bold Bathrooms www.boldbathroom.co.uk
Classic Rock Couture www.classicrockcouture.com
Clutterfingers www.clutterfingers.com
Deerstedt Lighting @deerstedt
Design Market www.design-market.eu
Discover Vintage www.discovervintageinteriors.co.uk
Dogwood Lifestyle www.dogwoodlifestyle.store
Earthen Forge www.earthenforge.com
Fabrication 78 www.etsy.com/shop/fabrication78
G Plan www.gplan.co.uk
Habitat www.habitat.co.uk
Heal's www.Heal's.com
Hologram House @thehologramhouse
IKEA www.IKEA.com
Isokon www.isokonplus.com
Jan Mlotkiewicz Restoration @retrorestorationuk
Kartell www.kartell.com
Kiwi Cakes @kiwicakesmanchester
Knoll www.knoll.com
Leopard Print Bee www.leopardprintbee.co.uk
Mathmos www.mathmos.com
Merrow Associates www.merrow-associates.com
Mid Century Traders www.midcenturytraders.com
Miracle Eye www.shopmiracleeye.com
Miss Pigeon Vintage www.misspigeonvintage.com
Mrs M. Vintage @mrsm.vintage
Neon Creations www.neoncreations.co.uk
Nick Reed Film Posters @nickreedfilmposters
Nine Lives Bazaar www.ninelivesbazaar.com
Paper Dress Vintage www.paperdressvintage.co.uk
Parker Knoll www.parkerknoll.co.uk
Pineapple Retro www.pineappleretro.co.uk

Plant Furniture www.plant.furniture
Pop Boutique www.pop-boutique.com
Potifiv www.potifiv.com
Rachel Goswell Glass www.rachelgoswellglass.com
Reclaim Queen www.reclaimqueen.co.uk
Retro Hauls @retrohauls
Retrospectrum www.retrospectrum.com.au
Ria Beer Vintage @riabeervintage
She is Eclectic www.ebay.co.uk/usr/she.is.eclectic
Snygg @snyggstyle
Sodastream www.sodastream.co.uk
Square Two Upholstery www.squaretwofurniture.co.uk
Squound @squound
The Furniture Rooms www.thefurniturerooms.co.uk
The Hippie Shake www.thehippieshake.co.uk
The Times Vintage www.thetimesvintage.com
Trafford Parsons www.traffordparsons.com
Vine Street Vintage @vinestreetvintage
Vitra www.vitra.com
Wreathcycled @wreathcycled
Yesterday People www.yesterdaypeople.com

Archives

V&A Archive vam.ac.uk/info/archives
High Wycombe Furniture Archive
hwfurniturearchive.bucks.ac.uk

DIY

Annie Sloane www.anniesloan.com
Faye Jennifer Vinyl Design www.fayejennifervinyldesign.co.uk
Vaspar www.valsparpaint.co.uk
Tru Tone Bulbs www.tru-tone.com

Entertainment

Barbarella @drinkswithbarbarella
Diffords www.diffordsguide.com
Meyer Dancers www.themeyerdancers.com

RESOURCES

Events

Modern Shows www.modernshows.com

Rose Bowl Flea Market www.rgcshows.com/rose-bowl

Long Beach California www.longbeachantiquemarket.com

Classic Car Boot Sale www.classiccarbootsale.co.uk

Back to Basics Events www.b2bevents.info

Discover Vintage Events www.discovervintageevents.co.uk

Brick Lane Market www.vintage-market.co.uk

Car boot sales directory www.carbootjunction.com

Further reading

Phaidon Design Classics Phaidon Editors

3-D Eye Michael English

70s Style & Design Dominic Lutyens, Kirsty Hislop

From A to Biba Barbara Hulanicki

Welcome to Big Biba Steven Thomas, Alwyn W Turner

The Original Pink Flamingos Don Featherstone,
  Tom Herzing

The House Book Sir Terence Conran

The Bed and Bath Book Sir Terence Conran

The Kitchen Book Sir Terence Conran

Kitsch Deluxe Lesley Gillilan

PAD Matt Maranian

PAD Parties Matt Maranian

Fat Lava Mark Hill

Just Above the Mantelpiece Wayne Hemingway

Pigeon's Luck Anthony Hocking and Vladimir Tretchikoff

The 70s House David Heathcote

Difford's Guide to Cocktails Simon Difford

Our True Intent Is All For Your Delight Martin Parr

Mid-Century Modern at Home D.C Hillier

The House Plant Expert Dr D.G Hessayon

Mid-Century Modern Design Dominic Bradbury

Decorative Art 70s Charlotte & Peter Fiell

Young Designs in Colour Barbara Plumb

Houses Architects Live In Barbara Plumb

Interior Decoration A-Z Betty Pepis

Bloomingdale's Book of Home Decorating
  Barbara Darcy

Your Beautiful Home on A Budget Alan Morgan

Planning Colour for Your Home Young Colour

How to Live in Style Young Colour

Additional photography credits

A huge thank you goes to the following fabulous humans who helped to make the book beautiful, I couldn't have done it without you – you are all truly special to me for the help that you gave me. **Laura Olden** – @savagehouse1970: 53, 93, 112, 142, 145. **Sarah Ransom** – @retro_saz: 45, 105, 107, 108, 113 above, 114 below, 129, 133. **Dann Fletcher** – @that.70s.chalet: 44, 129, 139, 159. **Natalie McCreesh** – @dogwoodlifestyle: 137. **Debbie Picken** – @bluelizardtextiles: 20, 41, 114. **Carrissa Leary** – @hendrix_and_willow: 66, 72, 73, 99, 111. **Larissa Blintz** – @houseofsunshine1967: 92. **David Freedman** – @the_avocado_lair: 86.

Kyle Books would like to acknowledge and thank the following for their help in supplying additional images for this book. Illustrations pages 46–49 by Evie Dunne. Photo Tony Feder 1, Photo Aldona Karczmarzyck 4, Benjamin Ashworth 20, Alamy Stock Photo Album/Paramount Pictures 24 above, Album/Thames Television 28, All Star Picture Library/Yorkshire Television/BBC 29, Everett Collection 170, Interfoto 25 above, 80, Marc Tielemans 60 above & below, 120, parkerphotography 41 above left, Peter Lopeman 26 below, Stockfolio 655 87, Terry Henshaw 77, Zuma Press 24 below; Design Council Archive, University of Brighton Design Archives. DCA-30-1-POR-B-BR-1 41 below right; Dreamstime.com Allan Clegg 26 above centre; Esto Ezra Stoller 52; Courtesy G Plan, www.gplan.co.uk 38; Getty Images CBS via Getty Images 79 below, Jean-Claude Deutsch/Paris Match 35 right, Justin de Villeneuve/Hulton Archive 35 left, Michael Ochs Archives 30 above, Popperfoto via Getty Images 37; via Knoll International 37 below right, Shutterstock ITV 76 above left, Kobal/Hemdale 31 below, Kobal/Universal Pictures 25 below, photolinc 79 above Roger Bamber 30 below; via Villeroy & Boch 81, Apollo Retro 37, Pyrex plates Theresa Morrissey Manship 88, Sideboard Benjamin Ashworth 98, Pieff Toby Thomas 125, Nathan Marie Dewaguet 122, Merrow James Young 128, Babycham Sophie Barnes 166.

INDEX

A

Aalto, Alvar 127
Aarnio, Eero 19, 66
Abigail's Party 29, 72, 170
air travel 26, 27
Allen, Jenni 40
animals: animal print 76
    ceramic animals 61
antiques markets 150
Are You Being Served? 28
areca palm 48
Argos 36
Arkana 66, 105
art 70–3, 142–7
art deco 20, 32
art nouveau 19
Ashley, Laura 20, 87
Athena 70, 143
auctions, local 150
avocados 161, 163
Axminster 116, 139–40

B

Babycham 166, 167
banana candle 165
Bardot, Brigitte 34
Barker, Ronnie 28
Bates, Fred, David
    and Tim 125
bathrooms 80–5
Bauhaus 57, 127
Baxter, Geoffrey 64
Beardsley, Aubrey 19
Beaver 39
bedrooms 92–5
Bejam 161
Benidorm 27
Bennett, R. 38
Bertoia, Harry 36
Bézier, Pierre 144
Biba 6–7, 9, 13, 20, 34–5, 70
Big Bud Press 157
birthday cakes 162
Blake, Peter 36
Blondie 169
Blumenthal, Heston 161
The Bold Bathroom
    Company 82
Boot's 70

bottle gardens 44
Bowie, David 30, 136
Bracegirdle, Arthur 68
Brampton, Sally 35
breeze blocks 118
Breuer, Marcel 36, 126–7
Briers, Richard 29
Brokenbog 82
Brown, Barbara 40
Brown, Craig 37
Broyhill 69
Bucknell, Barry 20, 54
Burke, Maurice 105
Butler, Ted 50
Butlin, Billy 77
Butlin's 27, 77

C

cakes 162, 164
California Cool 50
candlelight 134
car boot sales 151, 153
carpets, shag pile 20,
    101, 138–41
Carry On 29
Cauty, Jimmy 143
ceramics 56–9, 60, 61, 101,
132
chairs 19, 108
    Blofeld chair 121
    Cesca chair 36, 127
    garden 118
    Marcel Breuer's long
    chair 126–7
    Panton chair 66, 68, 118
    Parker Knoll Penshurst
    chair 20–1
    S-Chair Model 275 68
    swivel chairs 121
    Tulip chair 19, 69, 105
    wicker chairs 106
chandeliers 132
charity shops 151, 157
cheese fondue 165
chests of drawers 93
Chianti 166
Christensen, Ole 143
cladding, wood 93

Clappison, John 60
Classic Rock Couture 157
Cleese, John 28
A Clockwork Orange 72
clothing 148, 156–9
Cloudflare 136
cocktails 75, 166
Colani, Luigi 81
colour 19, 20, 97, 114–17
    60–30–10 rule 114
    bathrooms 80–1
    gardens 118
    space-age design 68
comedy 28
computers 24–5
Concorde 26, 27
Conran, Terence 21, 36–7,
    127, 134, 135
The Conran Shop 36, 135
conversation pits 52–3
cooks, television 162
Cooley, Dr Graham 57
Copeland, Greg 143
Corbett, Ronnie 128
Coronation Street 76
Courrèges, André 66
Cradock, Fanny 162, 165
crafts 19
Craigslist 151
Creda 86
Crestworth 136, 137
crewel embroidery 144
curtains 106, 114
cushions 106

D

Dartington Glass 64
Davis, Angela 24
Day, Lucienne 40
Denby 87
design, influential 34–41
Desso 140
Devil's ivy 46
disco 30, 82–5
Ditzel, Nanna 106
Dogwood Lifestyle 61, 140
The Doors 30
Dragon tree 46

dressing tables 93
Drexel 69, 92
drinks 166–7
Dunaway, Faye 95
Dunn, Clive 31

E

eBay 44, 151, 152
Eddington, Paul 29
Ege Rya 139, 140
English, Michael 143
Eno, Brian 30
entertaining 160–7
Ercol 122
Erzeugnis, Lusch 105
Esmonde, John 29
Estelle's Festive Fun
    Snowball 166
Etheridge, Pat 19
Etsy 44, 151

F

Fablon 54
fabrics 19, 20, 40, 115, 147
Facebook Marketplace
    69, 151
fairy lights 78
fashion 148, 156–9
Fat Lava 47
Fawlty Towers 28–9
Featherstone, Don 78
Ferrieri, Anna Castelli 68
fibre optics 25
Field, Michael 162
film 25
Finn, Fred 26
Fitz-Simon, Stephen 7, 34
flamenco dolls 77
flamingos 78, 118
Fleetwood Mac 30, 168
flokati rugs 101, 139
flowers, fake 78
folk-art wall hangings 144
food 160–5
Fortnum & Mason 64
Franco, General 27
Frenzy 70
fruit, fake 78

THANK YOU

Firstly, I would love to thank my fabulous publishing team at Kyle who let me run amok with writing a book about a subject I love, thank you for believing in me from day one, and trusting me to do my own thing with your precious pages, especially publisher Jo Copestick and the amazing Samhita Foria, without whom this project would not have come into existence. Thanks also to photographer Brent Darby, not only for making our home look wonderful, but for constant belly laughs and dodgy photographs of apples. Big shout out to Helen Bratby for pulling everything together and making the book look fabulous – we got there in the end!

There are so many people, who have supported me, not only with this project, but from the very beginning of my journey. I dedicate my first book with much love to my parents, Bob and Elaine, for nurturing me and educating me in not only good but bad design, and also for giving me a truly rounded education in all things weird and wonderful, and for never, ever doubting me and making sure I could wire a plug.

For Stephen, you saved me in ways only you and I know, and I love you all the more for it, thank you for your constant support, nagging and vacuuming, ability to ignore the tat that I constantly bring into our home and for always trusting my vision. To my darling Mouse, Lilly and Viki, you know who you are and I did promise to add you into the book, somewhere.

To my loyal friends, who have always had my back and pushed me to actually finish a project (for once), Nat, my aux brain, Inga the wise, and long-time TW, Rachel for inspiring me to create, CJ for decades of train chats and retro artwork, Alastair for enabling my tat habits, Amanda, Simon and Loggy for decades of love and not getting sick of me and finally Louise who always can be relied upon to rescue me in a crisis.

Special thanks also go to Barbara Hulanicki for not only agreeing to write the foreword and being a thoroughly good sport, but for the laughs and chats along the way, I never thought I would get to work with my hero.

To Scarlett Rickard without whom 70s House Manchester Shop would not even exist, you listen to my waffle and make magic happen with the designs you create for me – I wouldn't be where I am today without you.

To Claire at Griffin for artwork and amazing logos, Adam from Biba Boys, Jo from Kiwi Cakes for the amazing shag and hedgehog cakes, Tim from Squound, Fola from Square Two and Gemma from Barnado's, Cheadle, for allowing me to have photoshoots for the book.

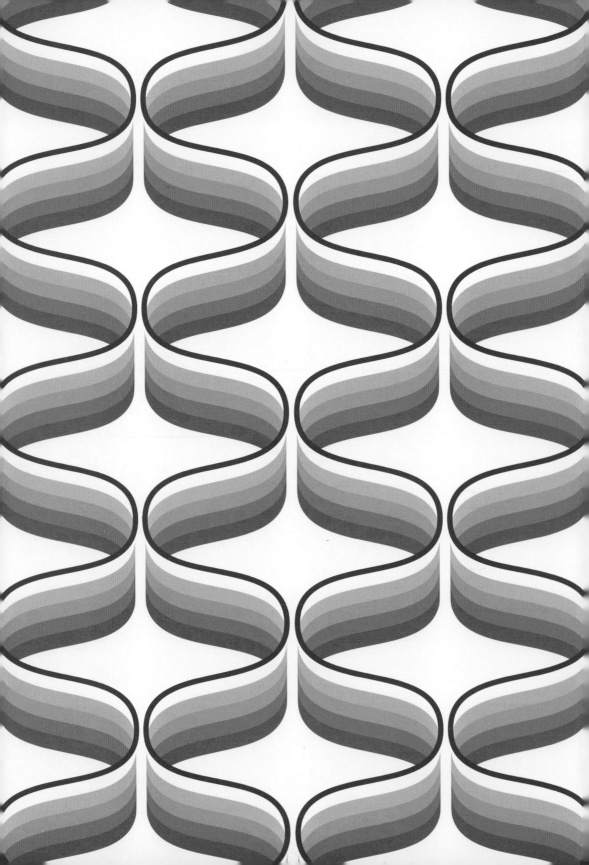